Truth Teller: The Price

Vernon Coleman

Books by Vernon Coleman include:

Medical
The Medicine Men
Paper Doctors
Everything You Want To Know About Ageing
The Home Pharmacy
Aspirin or Ambulance
Face Values
Stress and Your Stomach
A Guide to Child Health
Guilt
The Good Medicine Guide
An A to Z of Women's Problems
Bodypower
Bodysense
Taking Care of Your Skin
Life without Tranquillisers
High Blood Pressure
Diabetes
Arthritis
Eczema and Dermatitis
The Story of Medicine
Natural Pain Control
Mindpower
Addicts and Addictions
Dr Vernon Coleman's Guide to Alternative Medicine
Stress Management Techniques
Overcoming Stress
The Health Scandal
The 20 Minute Health Check
Sex for Everyone
Mind over Body
Eat Green Lose Weight
Why Doctors Do More Harm Than Good
The Drugs Myth

Complete Guide to Sex
How to Conquer Backache
How to Conquer Pain
Betrayal of Trust
Know Your Drugs
Food for Thought
The Traditional Home Doctor
Relief from IBS
The Parent's Handbook
Men in Bras, Panties and Dresses
Power over Cancer
How to Conquer Arthritis
How to Stop Your Doctor Killing You
Superbody
Stomach Problems – Relief at Last
How to Overcome Guilt
How to Live Longer
Coleman's Laws
Millions of Alzheimer Patients Have Been Misdiagnosed
Climbing Trees at 112
Is Your Health Written in the Stars?
The Kick-Ass A–Z for over 60s
Briefs Encounter
The Benzos Story
Dementia Myth
Waiting

Psychology/Sociology
Stress Control
How to Overcome Toxic Stress
Know Yourself (1988)
Stress and Relaxation
People Watching
Spiritpower
Toxic Stress
I Hope Your Penis Shrivels Up
Oral Sex: Bad Taste and Hard To Swallow
Other People's Problems

The 100 Sexiest, Craziest, Most Outrageous Agony Column
Questions (and Answers) Of All Time
How to Relax and Overcome Stress
Too Sexy To Print
Psychiatry
Are You Living With a Psychopath?

Politics
England Our England
Rogue Nation
Confronting the Global Bully
Saving England
Why Everything Is Going To Get Worse Before It Gets Better
The Truth They Won't Tell You...About The EU
Living In a Fascist Country
How to Protect & Preserve Your Freedom, Identity & Privacy
Oil Apocalypse
Gordon is a Moron
The OFPIS File
What Happens Next?
Bloodless Revolution
2020
Stuffed
The Shocking History of the EU
Coming Apocalypse
Covid-19: The Greatest Hoax in History
Old Man in a Chair
Endgame
Proof that Masks do more harm than Good
Covid-19: The Fraud Continues
Covid-19: Exposing the Lies
Social Credit: Nightmare on Your Street
NHS: What's wrong and how to put it right
They want your money and your life.
Their Terrifying Plan

Diaries and Autobiographies
Diary of a Disgruntled Man

Just another Bloody Year
Bugger off and Leave Me Alone
Return of the Disgruntled Man
Life on the Edge
The Game's Afoot
Tickety Tonk
Memories 1
Memories 2
Memories 3
My Favourite Books

Animals
Why Animal Experiments Must Stop
Fighting For Animals
Alice and Other Friends
Animal Rights – Human Wrongs
Animal Experiments – Simple Truths

General Non Fiction
How to Publish Your Own Book
How to Make Money While Watching TV
Strange but True
Daily Inspirations
Why Is Public Hair Curly
People Push Bottles Up Peaceniks
Secrets of Paris
Moneypower
101 Things I Have Learned
100 Greatest Englishmen and Englishwomen
Cheese Rolling, Shin Kicking and Ugly Tattoos
One Thing after Another

Novels (General)
Mrs Caldicot's Cabbage War
Mrs Caldicot's Knickerbocker Glory
Mrs Caldicot's Oyster Parade
Mrs Caldicot's Turkish Delight
Deadline

Second Chance
Tunnel
Mr Henry Mulligan
The Truth Kills
Revolt
My Secret Years with Elvis
Balancing the Books
Doctor in Paris
Stories with a Twist in the Tale (short stories)
Dr Bullock's Annals
The Awakening of Dr Amelia Leighton
A Needle for a Needle: A Mother's Covid Revenge

The Young Country Doctor Series
Bilbury Chronicles
Bilbury Grange
Bilbury Revels
Bilbury Country
Bilbury Village
Bilbury Pie (short stories)
Bilbury Pudding (short stories)
Bilbury Tonic
Bilbury Relish
Bilbury Mixture
Bilbury Delights
Bilbury Joys
Bilbury Tales
Bilbury Days
Bilbury Memories

Novels (Sport)
Thomas Winsden's Cricketing Almanack
Diary of a Cricket Lover
The Village Cricket Tour
The Man Who Inherited a Golf Course
Around the Wicket
Too Many Clubs and Not Enough Balls

Cat books
Alice's Diary
Alice's Adventures
We Love Cats
Cats Own Annual
The Secret Lives of Cats
Cat Basket
The Cataholics' Handbook
Cat Fables
Cat Tales
Catoons from Catland

As Edward Vernon
Practice Makes Perfect
Practise What You Preach
Getting Into Practice
Aphrodisiacs – An Owner's Manual
The Complete Guide to Life

Written with Donna Antoinette Coleman
How to Conquer Health Problems between Ages 50 & 120
Health Secrets Doctors Share With Their Families
Animal Miscellany
England's Glory
Wisdom of Animals

Dedicated to Antoinette
You live in my heart. I am always with you and
by your side and will never be away from you.

Introduction

Early in 2020, Antoinette and I realised that governments around the world were over-selling the risks associated with the coronavirus. Widely quoted predictions based on mathematical models were clearly outrageous, and everyone in government and the medical profession seemed to have forgotten that the ordinary, common or garden flu can (and does) kill many hundreds of thousands every year. The warnings and predictions were clearly exaggerated, and the epidemiology of what was being promoted as a new and deadly plague was clearly identical to the epidemiology of the annual flu. Neil Ferguson, the man most widely recognised as being behind the mathematical models had a terrible track record, and it was difficult to see why anyone in authority was taking any notice of his warnings. Ferguson was professor of mathematical biology at Imperial College in London and on the basis of his advice, the politicians decided we should be locked in and subjected to social distancing rules.

But this is what the Government knew about Ferguson when they decided to put their trust in him and his team:

In 2001, the Imperial team did the modelling on foot and mouth disease which led to a cull of six million sheep, pigs and cattle. The cost to the UK was around £10 billion. But the Imperial's work has been described as 'severely flawed'.

In 2002, Ferguson predicted that up to 50,000 people would die from mad cow disease. He said that could rise to 150,000 if sheep were involved. In the UK, the death total was 177.

In 2005, Ferguson said that up to 200 million people could be killed by bird flu. The total number of deaths was 282 worldwide. That's 282, not 282 million.

In 2009, Ferguson and his chums at Imperial advised the Government which, relying on that advice, said that swine flu would kill 65,000 people in the UK. In the end swine flu killed 457 people in the UK.

Finally, Ferguson admitted that his model of the covid-19 was based on undocumented 13-year-old computer code that was intended for use with an influenza epidemic.

No one seemed to question Ferguson's work on covid-19 – despite the fact that if he was wrong again (which I believed he was) the nation would be pushed back into the Dark Ages as a result of his work.

In February and March of 2020, I questioned the claim that we were at the start of a major plague. In the early months of 2020, I started writing articles for my websites about what I called then 'The Coronavirus Hoax'. I could see that bad things were about to happen and I knew I had to do whatever I could to share my fears with as many people as possible.

My comments (all of which were entirely accurate and based on fact) proved deeply unpopular with the medical and political establishment. Overnight, without any evidence, I was labelled as a conspiracy theorist, a discredited doctor and a danger to mankind. I believe that I was subsequently targeted more than anyone (and I know of no other doctor or author in the world who has been as completely banned as I have) and I suspect this was simply because I have a medical degree, a good deal of experience in writing and a large, global audience of loyal readers.

Twenty years previously, I'd been allotted a Wikipedia page (though I had frequently asked for it to be removed because it frequently contained errors of fact).

Suddenly the content of the page was dramatically changed with no reference to me and no respect for the facts.

All details of my books, TV series and columns were removed and replaced with lies and nonsense. (For example, the ASA is a private body which has not banned any advertising for any of my books. Indeed, it does not have the authority to ban anything and receives money from big advertisers, including drug companies.)

Wikipedia pages which had been put up about two of my book series (Mrs Caldicot and Bilbury) mysteriously disappeared. Google, which has a 'relationship' with Wikipedia, repeated the lies. It was clear this was all designed to make sure that no one took any notice of what I had to say. It was pretty clearly also designed to destroy me personally and to wreck my book sales. (One or two people have, I think, tried to restore sense to the pages. As far as I know no one has succeeded because the page appears to be mysteriously 'locked'.

)

Even the Wikipedia site relating to the award winning movie of my novel *Mrs Caldicot's Cabbage War* was deliberately wrecked. The film had terrific reviews, is regularly shown on TV and has over 1,000 reviews at nearly 5 stars on Amazon but Wikipedia now shows only a one star review from the BBC. My name has been removed from the summary box so that I'm not included on other derivative sites, and the only time I'm mentioned as the author, I'm described, inevitably, as a conspiracy theorist.

In my view, Wikipedia is a disinformation site, spreading misinformation and defending the indefensible. Wikipedia editors will remove the lies from a page if you give them money. Then, when it gets changed back, they want more money to tidy it up (I have emails proving that Wikipedia editors do this). I'm sure that sort of behaviour used to be against the law. At least one of the editors named as responsible for altering my Wikipedia page has, according to Larry Sanger (Wikipedia's co-founder), suspected links to the CIA.

With Wikipedia as the trigger, the trolls who patrol the internet clearly felt that I was fair game for any lies they wanted to invent. I was accused of spreading misinformation because the truth I was telling was considered inconvenient. I was wrongly accused (many times) of having been struck off the medical register. I was accused (many times) of falsely claiming to be a doctor. I was accused of making my videos to 'make money' though I had always refused to monetise them because I didn't want adverts in my videos. In reality, telling the truth cost me a great deal of money, several years of my life (at a point when time is the one commodity I'm short of), a destroyed reputation, a career in tatters and a constant stream of abuse.

(Incidentally, I haven't looked at `my' Wikipedia page for three years. I haven't looked because it will make me physically sick if I do. But I do have a fine collection of screenshots of libellous remarks made by 'editors' on the pages behind my Wikipedia entry.)

Four decades ago my books were reviewed in most national newspapers and magazines, in countries all around the world. That has changed.

Today my books are now never reviewed or serialised. Publishers in the UK and the US won't publish my books. I once had agents and publishers selling my books in 26 languages and just about every country in the world. I've now lost all those agents and publishers. I've had a number of books banned by independent online platforms.

It seems quite a price to pay just for telling the truth.

None of those who has banned me or attacked me or accused me of spreading misinformation have ever found any inaccuracies in anything I've written. I am widely libelled and sneeringly dismissed, without any evidence whatsoever, as a discredited conspiracy theorist.

One of the many things I've learned in recent years is that there is much truth in the saying 'no good deed goes unpunished'. Exposing the covid lies was something I did because it was the right thing to do – and because I had to do it. But the price has been almost unbearable.

Within a few months of starting to make videos for YouTube in March 2020, I was getting millions of views. I acquired well over 200,000 subscribers in record time.

(I should point out that making videos was not something with which I felt comfortable. I abandoned my television career many decades ago because I preferred writing to broadcasting and although I made a number of television series, I think I was pretty poor at television. I also hated the amount of time it took to travel to studios, hang around and then make a programme. But it was clear to us in early 2020 that in order to reach the maximum number of people, and to provide them with the warnings we felt were necessary, I would have to start making videos.)

Before long, however, YouTube started to take down videos. And then they removed my channel and banned me permanently. They even banned me from looking at other people's videos. Nothing in the videos I made was factually inaccurate. But YouTube doesn't seem to care about freedom or truth. The editors didn't seem to understand what they were doing. Even videos which didn't threaten the official line were removed. For example, early on I suggested that lockdown victims should take vitamin D supplements. YouTube censored, removed and banned the video. A month or so later, the British Government issued exactly the same warning.

I then put my videos on a platform called Brand New Tube. Within a short time the platform was told it would be shut down if they continued to host my videos. Bravely, Muhammad Butt, who ran the platform, took BNT abroad so that I could keep making videos.

I was refused permission to open a Facebook account or a Twitter account. My popular account on LinkedIn (which had not included anything about covid-19 or, indeed, anything about anything very much, for the simple reason that I found the site impossible to use) was suddenly closed without warning or explanation. I am not allowed any access to social media sites but fake sites have appeared in my name and are allowed to remain.

Those with accounts on social media quickly found that they were banned (temporarily or permanently) if they dared refer to, or worse still recommend, any of my videos, articles or books. If my videos or articles are put on sites such as YouTube by other people they are taken down within minutes. Many people admit that they won't put my videos on their Twitter or Facebook channels lest they be punished. On one occasion when I was invited to speak in public in 2021, the organiser had four venues cancelled.

My website had been hacked and attacked for decades but things got worse. For two years there have been at least 5,000 to 6,000 hacking attempts every month on the two main sites www.vernoncoleman.com and www.vernoncoleman.org. Occasionally, the websites have been taken down. My sites have been repeatedly shadow-banned and hidden (particularly by Google). In particular, I have been hacked by the Americans (including at least two of the various alphabet soup organisations), the Russians and the South Koreans though today most of the attempted hacking comes from Canada. (As I write, www.vernoncoleman.org is unavailable and has been so badly compromised that it will remain unavailable, though www.vernoncoleman.com survives for the moment.)

During the last two years, half a century of hard work and campaigning has been trashed and my reputation has been steadily destroyed by lies and libels on the internet and in the mainstream media. I was banned by all mainstream media, and TV and radio stations attacked me without giving me a right to reply. One national newspaper in the UK claimed that I was pretending to be a doctor. I have, inevitably, been threatened with legal action and I've received death threats.

Privately and professionally, sharing the truth in 2020 was the worst thing I ever did. It has brought me and my beloved, hard-working and constantly loyal wife nothing but personal and professional pain. It has taken up nearly every minute of my life for the best part of four years.

The aim of the attacks was not, simply to destroy me (though that was undoubtedly part of it), the aim was to stop people listening to anything I said, or reading anything I wrote. Before March 2020 I had many millions of readers around the world. I wonder how many I have left now. Precious few, I suspect. How do people know or care that the word 'discredited', plucked out of thin air and applied to my name by an unreliable encyclopaedia called Wikipedia, widely spread by that evil search engine Google, is just a libel and not a fact? It got to the point where we thought seriously that the only thing left was for the Government to send round a wet team to put bullets into our heads. And we were so depressed that we just rather hoped they did it cleanly and quickly.

And this sort of defamation doesn't just break and silence the individuals who are targeted – it also dissuades others from speaking out.

I was expelled from the Royal Society of Arts because 'of my views and my involvement in the BBC panorama programme'. That's what they said. This seemed to me to be a bit like arresting someone because they'd been mugged. I was never invited to appear on the programme they mentioned which was, inevitably, a one-sided 'hit' job, criticising those of us who were daring to tell the (provable) truth. The RSA didn't seem concerned that the BBC boasts that it won't ever give airtime to those questioning vaccination 'whether they're right or wrong'.

The abuse on social media grew and grew. It wasn't normal, unpleasant social media abuse. It was a campaign of suppression and oppression, decorated with malicious lies, invented and spread to cause doubt and to help keep the truth suppressed.

The ruthlessness and cruelty and refusal to debate are evidence of the fundamental wickedness. (I've frequently offered to debate with 'the other side' but all my challenges have been ignored.)

Someone watches everything I do. In May 2022, a publisher working outside the UK and the US finally produced an English language paperback version of my thrice banned book 'Covid-19: The Greatest Hoax in History'. I mentioned the book's publication on my website. Within hours the publisher's PayPal account was closed making it difficult for him to sell books by mail order. He then opened another payment account with a different company and, almost immediately, that account was also closed.

And on it goes. There is much more but I expect you are as bored with reading this sorry tale as I am of writing it.

Everything I've written was absolutely accurate, and time and time again my predictions have been correct. In reality it hasn't been difficult to work out what would happen next. (The videos I've made for BNT are still available on www.onevsp.com and on www.BitChute.com and other sites and the transcripts of my YouTube videos are available in books and on my websites. I stand by everything I said and wrote. And, indeed, after the first one, my videos were always scripted to make sure that I had a hard copy of what I'd said and to make sure that every fact and reference I gave had been carefully checked.)

I tell you all this to show just how bad things have become, how the truth is suppressed and how truth-tellers are mercilessly and ruthlessly demonised.

And remember: my accusers and detractors will never debate with me. They are not interested in the truth – only in propaganda.

I suspect that there are still many people who, although aware that the so-called pandemic was a fake, and who are aware that the whole covid-19 fraud was part of something much larger (a complex and long-standing plot which I described in my book *Their Terrifying Plan*) are not aware that what is happening now has been tried before – though, admittedly, on a smaller scale.

To understand how, when and why we need to go back to the Second World War.

It is generally, and wrongly, assumed that Adolf Hitler devised the murderous ideology for which he is now most remembered: the relentless killing of millions of men, women and children who were considered to be too imperfect (in some judgemental way) to be allowed to live.

But the idea of mass sterilisation, which morphed into genocide, did not originate with Hitler or any of the leading members of the National Socialist Party.

The idea of turning eugenic theory into a practical mission to purify the German race originated with the medical profession.

It was, I'm afraid, medical doctors who came up with the idea of removing the weak from society – whether they be physically or mentally disabled or of the 'wrong' religion. The 'cleansing' of the German people was not originally or primarily a Nazi programme and it was not simple anti-Semitism. (The removal of Jews and gypsies was just one part of the purification process.)

It was doctors who encouraged the Nazis to regard disease as a purely social problem rather than a result of external influences such as infections, and it was German doctors who promoted an early and particularly toxic version of social credit. Those who were promoting the German eugenics programme didn't simply kill people for not marching the correct way, giving the right salutes and singing the proper songs (all attributes which would, they seemed to suggest, imply a long and healthy life) but they also chose to kill anyone who didn't look acceptable to them. Anyone whom they thought looked 'odd' or 'ugly' would be killed since if they got into the wrong beds they might endanger the purity of the species.

(There is no little irony in the fact that the German doctors responsible for this very particular form of genocide did not exactly look handsome or endearing. Most of them looked like ugly, scary versions of over the top baddies in a World War II film. You can see photos of some of the doctors in the excellent but chilling documentary entitled 'Action T4: A Doctor under Nazism'.)

And what is frightening is that what happened in Germany in the 1920s and 1930s is now happening throughout the world.

The globalists, aided and abetted by the medical profession, are determined to rid the world of the elderly, the disabled, the weak and the mentally ill. And they are doing it more efficiently, more ruthlessly and more effectively than the German doctors who led Hitler and the Nazis into their programme of genocide.

In 1933, in Germany, the Nazis introduced a Law for the Prevention of Hereditarily Diseased Offspring. The law ruled that any person would be considered as hereditarily diseased if they were suffering from any one of the following diseases: congenital mental deficiency, schizophrenia, manic-depressive insanity, hereditary epilepsy, hereditary chorea (Huntington's), hereditary blindness, hereditary deafness and any severe hereditary deformity. It was also decided that any person suffering from severe alcoholism may also be rendered incapable of procreation.

Deciding to kill lots of people was one thing, of course. Putting the killing into practice was something else and in Germany, before the Second World War, doctors who had been deeply influenced by the principles of eugenics spent much time trying to work out the best way to get rid of the disabled, the elderly and the weak, and they worked hard to try to find a solution which they could 'sell' to Hitler, the rest of the medical profession, the nation as a whole and, most of all, themselves.

The doctors behind the mass slaughter wanted a self-righteous, medical answer to what they regarded as a huge threat – the existence of people whom they regarded as a drag on society; people who took rather than gave; people who were dependent on others and who cost a good deal to keep alive.

Many people (particularly the elderly and infirm) were killed by being starved to death. (This simple procedure has remained popular around the world for some decades. Visit any modern hospital and you will see elderly patients being starved to death.) In the end they settled on using carbon monoxide gas to kill their 'patients', but in order to keep up appearances, hide what they were doing and, perhaps, to appease what was left of their consciences, they pretended that the gas chambers were part of a treatment process.

(This self- serving philosophy was followed when the deadly covid-19 vaccination programme was introduced. Doctors pretended that the vaccine was designed to provide protection against a deadly disease, although the evidence shows that the product appears to have been designed not to protect or to cure but to kill.)

The gas chambers were originally designed not as the infamous showers but as 'inhalation rooms' where patients could inhale what they were told was a 'medicinal' gas for their health. Special treatment rooms were set up where 'patients' could be brought in by train and bus to be 'treated'.

Immediately after their 'treatment', the bodies of the murdered patients would be incinerated and their ashes dumped in a nearby river.

Naturally, the Germans wanted to cover the costs of their enterprise and so they removed gold teeth and sent the gold off to the Bank for International Settlements in Switzerland (BIS). The BIS then handed the money over to the Nazis. The doctors also removed the brains from the corpses and handed them to a neurologist to play with. I use the words 'play with' deliberately since the 'research' which was done produced no useful results.

Finally, the ruthless Germans had another money-making trick. They pretended that their 'patients' were still alive so that they could claim from the State or from relatives for the cost of their medical care. The doctors and bureaucrats in charge of the killing proudly worked out how much money they were saving Germany by killing people who consumed rather than produced.

It is worth noting that the doctors working in this unusual field of medicine were very well paid and a few decades later, when the covid-19 vaccine was introduced, the doctors who agreed to jab their patients with the unproven, experimental product were also extremely well paid for the efforts – being paid far more per vaccination than they were being paid for other vaccines.

This ruthless search for racial purity led the doctors into looking for ways to eradicate all those – such as Jews and gypsies – whom they regarded as a danger to the purity of the Aryan race. This was, almost certainly, the first time in history when doctors had cold-bloodedly plotted to kill their patients, and it seems that even the Nazi high command must have been shocked for at one point, Hitler deliberately distanced himself from the programme (originally called T4 and later known by the code name 14F15.). Even he was presumably alarmed by what the doctors were doing (or maybe he was merely alarmed by the public relations consequences of what he was doing).

Why have I bought this up? Why am I writing about this now?

The answer is that doctors around the world are now doing exactly what German doctors were doing in Nazi Germany. The only difference is that they are doing it more efficiently, more cold-bloodedly and on a much larger scale. The plan this time is not to kill off a few million people, killing them with gas, but to use a wide variety of methods to kill several billion in bulk. The German doctors who shocked even Hitler with their ruthlessness would be thrilled and delighted by the activities of the world's medical profession today.

It is worth noting that at the Nuremburg trials, doctors were judged to be guilty of war crimes if they experimented on patients without asking and obtaining their permission. Since the covid-19 vaccine was and is experimental, all the doctors who gave the vaccine without telling their patients that the vaccine was experimental, and then duly obtaining their permission, were and are guilty of war crimes.

Those doctors were, of course, also in breach of the Hippocratic Oath which contains the famous phrase 'First, do no harm'.

(Sadly, most medical schools and disciplinary bodies around the world (including the General Medical Council in the UK) have abandoned the Hippocratic Oath as out-dated.)

Here are some of the ways in which modern doctors have turned themselves into ruthless killing machines.

First, doctors introduced something called the Liverpool Care Pathway – a misnamed programme if ever there was one. The Liverpool Care Pathway doesn't have anything to do with 'care'. It is an officially approved programme which encourages doctors to kill their patients by denying them food and water. Patients (usually elderly) are literally starved to death. It sounds too awful to be true but you can check it out if you don't believe me. The fake pandemic which started in 2020 proved beyond question that governments everywhere want to kill their elderly citizens. In the UK, the Government actually boasted about the amount of money it was saving because of the number of elderly pensioners who had died (or, more accurately, 'exterminated').

Second, the global programme of medically approved lockdowns (whereby people were locked in their homes and the elderly were kept confined in care homes, without being allowed any visitors) made it very easy for doctors to kill the elderly. The officially approved plan was to allow doctors to get rid of the elderly in care homes. The absence of visitors made this exceptionally easy.

Third, BMA doctors announced that the profession should cut back on diagnosing and treating patients in order to reduce the 'carbon footprint of health care'. Absurdly, it was announced by senior figures within the medical establishment that doctors were helping patients too much and should cut back. There was even a suggestion that less anaesthetic should be used during surgery to save the planet from global warming (a pseudo-scientific phenomenon which has never been proven to exist and which is questioned by the majority of thinking scientists). The official excuse (and there is always an excuse) is that 'over-diagnosis is increasing the carbon footprint of health care'. Cutting back on patient care means that in the UK, doctors working in general practice now work an average 20-25 hours a week and the vast majority refuse to provide night time or weekend cover for their patients. Many doctors in general practice refuse to see patients at all on the bizarre and entirely self-serving grounds that if they see patients face to face they might catch an infection from them. The result is that most people who fall ill try to get themselves to the nearest Accident and Emergency department in a local hospital, where they may well wait a day or even more to be seen and treated. The ambulance service cannot cope with demands and patients have been known to wait 10 or 12 hours or even more for an ambulance to collect them. Moreover, to make things even worse, the British Medical Association (a trade union which represented doctors' financial interests and which I have for decades described as the patients' enemy) has instigated a number of strikes with doctors demanding a pay rise of 35% (or even more) even though the striking doctors must have known that such a pay rise could not possibly be paid. The result of the strikes is that in the summer of 2023, most of the patients dying in Britain were on waiting lists for essential treatment, and waiting lists were so long that it was recognised that most patients would probably die long before they were seen by a doctor. (Hospitals were having to pay striking doctors £7,900 per shift to stand in for themselves.) It seems to me that the BMA is determined to destroy the NHS, destroy health care in the UK, bring down the Government, kill as many people as possible and take the entire country, screaming or not, into the Great Reset. (Health care in all countries is now a very bureaucratic business, and I can think of a dozen ways in which doctors could go on strike and cause problems for the Government without affecting patients directly.) In autumn 2023, the leader of the Liberal Democrats promised that if his party gained power (not very likely it has be said) then they would guarantee that anyone referred for cancer treatment would be seen in two months. Putting aside the fact that a promise of an appointment within two months is scandalously unambitious for a patient with cancer, the Liberal Democrats don't seem aware that hospitals are very skilled at getting round targets. Patients will doubtless be 'seen' within two months, but when will their tests or treatment start? And will the person who 'sees' them merely be a receptionist? (Even those patients who were lucky enough to get into a hospital weren't all that well off. One poor woman felt so neglected that she had to resort to ringing 999 from her hospital bed.)

Fourth, doctors and nurses were widely reported to be encouraging patients to accept 'Do Not Resuscitate' notices on their medical records. Patients were told that resuscitation could be a painful procedure and that it might be better for them if they were merely allowed to die, rather than being saved. Nurses as well as doctors were allowed to 'sell' this idea to patients, and the individuals whose records were marked with DNR notices included young mentally ill and disabled patients. Men and women with Down 's syndrome have been widely labelled with DNR notices. (I am surprised that campaigners, charities and parents haven't complained more about what is happening. Maybe they have campaigned but have no voice. Heaven knows, it has been nigh on impossible for anyone questioning the globalists and their agenda to obtain any media coverage.)

Fifth, doctors all around the world agreed to give their patients an untested, experimental product which had been proved to do far more harm than good. The doctors giving the covid-19 vaccine were paid huge sums of money (far more than was usually paid for vaccination programmes) and so most ignored their ethical responsibilities and went along with the instructions which they were given by politicians and drug companies. Doctors who attempted to question the safety, efficacy or need for the covid-19 vaccination programme were demonised, monstered and attacked mercilessly. Most doctors who questioned the official line were described as 'conspiracy theorists' with some having the word 'discredited' as a bonus. (There is no little irony in the fact that some of the doctors who were openly critical of the truth-tellers have woken up, are speaking out and are now finding out how painful and damaging it can be to tell the truth in a time of suppression.) The evidence strongly suggests to me that the covid-19 vaccine was designed, marketed and given in order to kill rather than protect. Apart from the short-term dangers of the covid-19 jab (myocarditis, heart disease, blood clots and neurological problems for example) there is little doubt that the mRNA vaccine does massive harm to the

immune system of patients. There are also serious questions about
the long-term effect of the vaccine on the fertility of both female and
male patients. And, as I showed in a video early on in the campaign
to vaccinate everyone, there is evidence that the covid-19 vaccine
may have a dramatic and damaging effect on the human brain.
Doctors who were getting very rich allowed themselves to accept the
lies they were told in order to excuse their crimes against humanity.
And most doctors completely closed their minds to all the evidence.
I spoke to one medical consultant who argued vehemently that
covid-19 had killed millions of people and that the death rate in the
UK had increased massively because of covid-19. He was so
committed to the myth that he steadfastly refused to change his mind
even when I pointed out that the Government's own figures proved
him quite wrong.

Sixth, it has become routine in hospitals and care homes for
doctors to 'treat' patients who are elderly, frail or in need of medical
and nursing support with a 'kill shot' consisting of a lethal mixture
of morphine and a benzodiazepine tranquilliser. Since staff now do
not have to ask permission before giving tranquillisers to elderly
patients, the 'kill shot' can be administered to patients quite freely. It
is the modern equivalent of the gas chamber, and no amount of
protesting from the medical establishment will change this fact of
life (or should that be 'fact of death').

Seventh, medically backed and promoted euthanasia has become
a global phenomenon. In numerous countries around the world,
euthanasia programmes have been introduced in order to eliminate
the elderly and the sick by encouraging them to end their lives. (Life,
it seems, is imitating art for in 1953, Evelyn Waugh wrote a novel
called *Love Among the Ruins* in which he described a state-run
euthanasia centre.) In Trudeau's Canada, the Government has
introduced a very forceful euthanasia programme called 'medical
assistance in dying'. There were 13,000 state sanctioned 'suicides' in
Canada in 2022 and that country is now deciding whether to allow
children and the mentally ill to kill themselves. Please read that
sentence again. In Canada, euthanasia was introduced several years
ago and is proving very popular with doctors, bureaucrats and
politicians. A woman in Canada was recently offered a place on her
nation's euthanasia programme because of the delay involved in
having a stair lift fitted in her home. It was also reported that a

Canadian man who was facing eviction from social housing had been accepted onto the country's euthanasia program. CBC reported that medically assisted deaths could save millions in health care spending, and it was estimated that the savings 'exceedingly outweigh the estimated $1.5 million to $14.8 million in direct costs associated with implementing medically assisted dying'. The report judged that doctor-assisted death could reduce annual health care spending across Canada by between $34.7 million and $136.8 million. (Just how can anyone take a report seriously when the figures are so vague?) In the Netherlands, healthy individuals with autism are allowed the option of euthanasia, and Australia is deciding whether to let children as young as 14 kill themselves (or allow someone to do it for them). Today, euthanasia is legal in Belgium, Canada, Luxembourg, Netherlands, New Zealand, Spain, Columbia and parts of Australia. Globally, there is a state sanctioned epidemic of euthanasia as governments follow instructions from the conspirators and encourage more and more people to commit suicide.

Eighth, doctors are enthusiastically giving a live but attenuated flu vaccine to children. It is important to remember that although attenuated, the virus in these vaccines can become live. It is very possible, therefore, that children will transmit the infection to elderly relatives whose immune systems have been severely damaged by the covid-19 vaccinations they have been given. (Not a few elderly individuals have been given six covid-19 vaccinations – at great profit to their doctors.)

Ninth, during the early days of the fake covid pandemic, autopsies were halted. Allegedly, this was done to protect pathologists who might otherwise be at risk of catching the flu from their dead patients. It was done to hide the fact that people who had allegedly died of covid had in truth died of something else. It was also done to create more fear and to enhance the lie that we were facing a deadly plague. (The risk was surely very slight since the flu is usually spread by coughing or sneezing and it is rare, even in these strange days, for dead patients to do much coughing or sneezing.)

Tenth, the United Nations has for some years now excluded the over 70-year-olds from its health statistics. Doctors can now kill as many over 70s as they like without any risk that their country's health care will be downgraded.

It is worth remembering that Nazi doctors pretended that they were 'helping' or 'treating' their patients when they gassed them. Today, doctors have done exactly the same thing. It is frightening to realise how many doctors do not realise how far down the slippery path they have already travelled. It's an easy route to take. Before they knew what they were doing, German doctors were opening the valves and killing people a score or more at a time. Today, doctors around the world happily endorsed, promoted and gave a toxic experimental drug which did not do what it was said to do but which did kill people.

The end result is that doctors today have compromised or abandoned their professional and personal responsibilities and have become members of a conspiracy, a cabal of murderous scientists. The best that can be said in their defence is that many are merely ignorant and are simply taking the money they are offered without asking any inconvenient questions.

The excuse they offer, that they are simply doing what they have been told to do by their government, is frighteningly reminiscent of the excuse offered by doctors (and others) who worked in the Nazi death camps.

Anyone who knows, or even suspects, what is going on but does not say anything is as guilty of the crimes being committed as the apologists and collaborators were in Nazi Germany.

I would argue that what is happening today is more blatant, more redolent of evil, than anything that happened in Germany in the 1940s.

These are the darkest of dark times.

And, of course, those telling the truth continue to be censored, banned and demonised.

Doctors and nurses have been forbidden to question the official line – even when the official line is patently wrong. If the Government says that everyone should consume eight gallons of custard a day then it is forbidden to question that statement. Doctors and nurses have been banned from speaking to the media unless they say the right thing. In September 2023, it was made illegal for any citizen in

Britain to question anything the Government said. Check out the Online Safety Bill if you don't believe me. Of course, the Bill hasn't been sold to the public as a way for the Government to suppress free speech. It has been sold as a way to protect the public.

I really shouldn't have been surprised at how I was censored, banned and demonised. Nothing that happened to me was really new – there was just a lot more of it than there had been previously.

I have, I suppose, always looked at life from the outside looking in.

I know when I became a rebel.

In 1964, at the age of 18, I went to Kirkby, Liverpool to spend a year as a Community Service Volunteer. I'd just left school and was taking a year off before going to medical school.

I arrived in Liverpool as a schoolboy, in a school blazer, tie and flannels. I spent my time there helping old people and working with an army of teenage school-children. I organised groups of teenagers to tidy gardens, paint flats and do shopping for lonely, housebound people.

Nine months later, I had seen more of life than I'd seen in the previous 18 years. I had become a professional rebel – fighting for freedom and human rights and against injustices of all kinds.

When I started medical school, I carried on working with 'lost' teenagers in Birmingham. I recruited a couple of gangs and got the members to help me run a night-club in a disused warehouse in the city centre so that kids had somewhere to go in the evenings. I borrowed an epidiascope and showed histology slides upside down on the ceiling (they looked pretty good) and because we didn't have any chairs, I took delivery of a pile of unwanted bedsteads and mattresses and had them placed around the side of the hall we used. Most of the gang members carried knives and were a little feisty to start with. And then I started carrying a Victorian swordstick with a three foot blade.

I wrote a number of national newspaper and magazine columns while I was at medical school and contributed features to publications as varied as *The Spectator* and the *Times Educational*

Supplement. I also reviewed plays and books for *The Birmingham Post*. I confess I spent much of the 1960s and 1970s writing articles and columns which were critical of the establishment.

And to begin with, the establishment was moderately tolerant.

My early books such as *The Medicine Men* and *Paper Doctors*, (both published in the 1970s) were widely praised in the national press. *The Guardian* newspaper bought serial rights for the first and published a huge extract. The BBC made a lengthy programme about the book for the early evening BBC1 news programme.

During the 1970s and early 1980s, while working as a GP in an English provincial town, I worked a good deal for both broadsheet and tabloid newspapers and for national TV stations. I wrote numerous columns and made several thousand TV and radio programmes. And I wrote a host of books which were mostly very well received and reviewed – appearing in the best-seller lists around the world. I was sued and served with injunctions and so on but that seemed to go with the territory.

My medical career came to an end in the 1980s when I was fined by the NHS because I refused to put diagnoses on sick notes. I felt that maintaining patient confidentiality was important. I resigned as a GP, though my protest resulted in a change in the regulations.

But then, at the end of the 1980s, there was a not very subtle change in the way the establishment treated original thinking: anyone who questioned the 'official' line was either actively suppressed or attacked. Any questioning of vaccination or vivisection, for example, drew violent attacks from the medical establishment and, in particular, from the pharmaceutical industry.

I was sued by all sorts of people. (And I sued a chief constable. I seem to remember trying to sue a judge too.) Most of the lawsuits I had to deal with were, I suspect, more to cause annoyance and waste my time. Because of my opposition to vivisection, I had MI5 and private detectives (hired by drug companies) chasing me and tracking me down. My mail was opened and insiders told me that Special Branch had a growing file about me. I was 'door stepped' by journalists on more occasions than I like to remember. I was regularly filmed by police forces. I received writs so thick that they wouldn't fit through the letter box and had to be pushed through a cat flap. I've had papers relating to drug companies stolen from my home. And, of course, my phone has been tapped for years. (I thought it rather comical when a former head of MI6 complained that the Russians had been reading his personal emails. The Secret Service admitted years ago that they'd been tapping phones and reading emails.)

I made a number of networked TV and radio series, wrote a column for the *Daily Star* for a decade and was *The Sun* doctor for another decade. Then I wrote the agony column for *The Sunday People* for yet another decade. I wrote columns under other names too.

But bit by bit the authorities started to haul in the net.

I was banned in China where the Chinese Government was so annoyed by a weekly column I wrote for a big Chinese newspaper that they banned all my books in Chinese and also banned other 'foreign' authors. (I was a bestselling author in China and wrote a weekly column for a Chinese newspaper). The column which caused the fuss was one in which I criticised vaccination.

In the UK, I was banned from speaking to NHS staff because it was felt that I would be a threat to the pharmaceutical industry. I had been booked to speak about drug side effects at a large conference but I was replaced by a drug company representative, and the conference was altered to put the blame for drug side effects onto patients rather than doctors or drug companies.

I resigned from my last national newspaper column in 2003 after the editor refused to publish an article I had written criticising the Iraq war. (On reflection that was undoubtedly a mistake. I should have hung on and used the column for other campaigns.)

A serious death threat was investigated for many months by the police and by Interpol, and when I travelled to South Africa to speak against vivisection, I was met by an agent of BOSS (the South African secret service) within hours of arriving in Johannesburg. (He wasn't terribly good at it. He turned up in a silk suit claiming to be an anti-vivisection activist and wanted to know everything about 'my friend ALF'. He didn't realise ALF was an organisation not a person.)

After I exposed the way the AIDS 'crisis' had been exaggerated, I found that I was no longer invited to contribute to TV or radio programmes. And publishers around the world suddenly let my books go out of print or remaindered them – and refused to consider new titles. A German publisher had been selling large amounts of my books but my books disappeared overnight. The publishers did not respond when I asked for royalty statements. That cost me a considerable sum a year in royalties – and a lot of readers in Germany. Much the same sort of thing happened around the world.

Book contracts were suddenly withdrawn and TV companies cancelled invitations. Publishers suddenly decided that they didn't want books they'd been keen to buy. By the late 1990s, for no discernible reason, unpleasant articles about me started to appear in the national press. A nasty and inaccurate piece about me appeared in *The Spectator*. It was commissioned by Boris Johnson and written by his sister. (There were so many errors that *The Spectator* had to publish a letter of correction.) The Independent and The Independent on Sunday published four profiles that are probably best described as unflattering.

And then, suddenly, it was 2020 and freedom of speech became something other people enjoyed.

Propaganda is of little real use if critics are allowed to question the claims that were being made and the techniques being used to deceive and manipulate. And so, after March 2020, telling the truth became a crime. The authorities decided that the truth was a dangerous commodity.

It was decreed that criticisms must be suppressed and censored and since that alone might not be enough, that the authors of all criticisms must be silenced, demonised, monstered, marginalised, lied about and destroyed so that no one listened to anything they had to say. And, of course, all this had to be done at the same time as the public were misdirected and fed an unrelenting diet of misinformation and disinformation.

From early 2020 onwards this was done with unprecedented ruthlessness, with the BBC in the lead as a supplier of misinformation and disinformation. And, of course, there was NO debating of the most important issues. The mainstream media was instructed not to interview those who questioned the fraud and conspiracy – but to allow unlimited airtime to those supporting the lies and the misinformation.

And at the same time governments, through the medium of their taxpayer funded security services, spread abuse and misinformation to marginalise and destroy experts who spoke out in an attempt to counter the lies.

When the internet was originally born there were some who thought that it would offer complete freedom. It now seems laughable that Google's corporate motto used to be 'First do no evil'. Google and its subsidiary YouTube, have become among the most fascist, evil, censorious and oppressive media organisations in the world – totally opposed to free speech.

(But Google was always an evil company and I suspect that the original motto was nothing but a promotional gimmick. The House of Commons Work and Pensions Committee singled out Google for continuing to run adverts for scammers while at the same time running adverts on how to avoid being scammed.)

Today, I would guess that 90% of the material about me on the internet is untrue. For Google and Wikipedia the percentage is much higher. The other 10% is mostly simply distorted. If this is remotely true for the rest of the material on the internet it means that the internet as a whole is entirely untrustworthy as a source of information. I haven't looked at Wikipedia for a long time (and to protect my sanity I shall never look again) but I have little doubt that by now that disreputable source of misinformation and disinformation is reporting that I was Jack the Ripper in Victorian England, responsible for the South Sea Bubble, the brains behind the Great Train Robbery and responsible for hideous war crimes during both the First and Second World Wars.

Many people believed that it was a victory when historian David Irving was sent to prison for questioning the extent of the holocaust.

But, ironically, it was a victory for fascism and oppression and it was the beginning of a journey down a very slippery slope. Irving's crime was to share an opinion and to tell the truth as he saw it and this was undoubtedly offensive to many who believed that he was wrong but the principle of free speech, long championed, was ignored in an attempt to silence uncomfortable opinions and to appease those who were offended.

Today, whistle blowing is a dangerous and destructive business.

Mainstream journalists always complain loudly whenever their colleagues are arrested or subjected to any form of censorship but writers trying to share truths about global warming and covid have been systematically oppressed and censored without any protest from journalists' groups.

Editors and journalists are making a big fuss over what are called Slapps (Strategic lawsuits against public participation). These are libel or privacy cases brought by wealthy people or companies to harass, intimidate and ultimately silence journalists and publishers. But at least these cases are out in the open.

The sad fact is that during the last three years (or, in my case, many more years) mainstream journalists have helped to suppress the truth and to cancel all scientific debate. The BBC has actually boasted that it does not give airtime to anyone who questions vaccination – 'whether they are right or wrong'. And this, it seems, is now acceptable. An author who writes a book on a controversial subject is likely to find it blasted everywhere with anonymous one star reviews before a copy has been sold. It is not uncommon for the authors of those one star reviews to boast that they haven't bought, looked at or read the book in question.

Moreover, whereas the police have often appeared to protect or assist global warming and Black Lives Matter protestors, protests about the fake pandemic and the global warming hoax have been heavily policed.

I was targeted the minute I put my head above the parapet and defined the coronavirus scare as a hoax. I was targeted in part because when the conspirators had previously tried to begin a scare campaign (with the AIDS scare back in the 1980s) I had been the one who had debunked the scare. For over half a century I had been attacking drug companies and the medical establishment; drawing attention to dangerous drugs. As a result I quickly became almost certainly the most banned individual in the world.

I have always preferred to speak out than to keep silent – even when it has been damaging.

I resigned as a GP because the NHS would not allow me to protect the confidentiality of my patients. I enjoyed looking after patients but I refused point blank to dump my principles out of the window just because NHS bureaucrats told me that I should. I had chosen to take the Hippocratic Oath when I qualified as a doctor and, unlike the entire medical establishment, I still took it seriously.

And I resigned from a column I wrote for *The People* for ten years between 1993 and 2003. It was a painful decision on several levels. For one thing they paid me a great deal of money. More importantly, I had a soap box from which to address important issues and reach several million people (at that time *The People's* circulation was considerably higher than it is now, and was measured in millions rather than thousands). I described this resignation in my book *People Push Bottles up Peaceniks* - the title refers to a famous *Daily Mirror* headline from the Second World War which ran 'British Army Push Bottles up Germans'. (Curiously, this appears to be just about the only book of mine which is no longer available second hand – though around ten thousand copies were printed, they all seem to have disappeared. I attempted to produce a reprint but found that quite impossible.)

In that book I pointed out that: 'In most cowboy movies which are set in a wild frontier town, there are half a dozen essential buildings. There's a saloon, bank and hotel; a sheriff's office (together with its inbuilt jail), a hardware store and newspaper office. The newspaper is usually run by a grizzled, slightly grumpy old man who publishes, edits and writes the paper virtually single-handedly. He may have a trusty assistant who lays out the type and gets shot early on. Apart from being the father/grandfather or uncle of the beautiful girl who provides the good guy with his romantic interest, the newspaperman is there as a standard bearer for truth, goodness and everything that is noble. He it is who fights the local bad guy – the greedy landowner, the psychopathic bad guy. At some point, around a third of the way into the movie, the newspaperman usually dies. But his fight for justice lives on. It may be naive of me, but when I first started writing for newspapers the grizzled old newspaper editor and proprietor in that western town was my hero. He courageously brought out his paper denouncing the bad guy regardless of the risks. He cared passionately for the truth and his mission in life was to share the truth (and his opinions of the truth) with the reading public. Nothing – no threats, no bribes and no guns – could silence him. He exposed crooked politicians and bullying landowners with the same even handedness. He was concerned only with two things: truth and justice.'

When I was young I loved that newspaperman. (And, indeed, I still do.) He was, I thought, what journalism was all about: courage, integrity and a firm belief in justice and the freedom of the press.

I've always felt that newspapers should be about justice, freedom and truth. Sadly, although that may have been true, once upon a time, it hasn't been true for a very long time.

Fighting the misinformation has been a full time job for both of us. For the best part of three years my wife Antoinette and I worked every hour available to dig out information to help counter the lies that were being told by governments, government advisors and journalists.

We were invariably the first to issue warnings about the fake pandemic and its associated frauds.

Throughout 2020, I warned about compulsory vaccination, the very real health risks associated with the proposed lockdowns, the health risks associated with masks and hand sanitisers (both dramatically under-estimated problems), the horrors of DNR notices, the uselessness of the PCR test, and the way it could be used to collect DNA samples, and the side effects and dangers of the covid-19 jabs. I warned about the fake disease 'long covid' and was the first to draw attention to the rise in cancer cases among those who had received the covid jab. I warned that if the 'vaccine' were given straight into a blood vessel (by mistake) then the side effects could be far more serious. I warned about the end of cash a decade or more ago.

I never charged people to access my websites, I never monetised my DVDs, I never asked for money from those who watched videos or copied videos or articles for their own sites. I relied on my income from books to pay the cost of running my websites (it cost me well over £10,000 just to keep two websites running and to purchase books and so on to do the necessary research). The blocking and the censorship meant that my book sales fell by 75% to 80% – devastating my income.

At the same time I was demonised but I was unable to defend myself on social media (where much of the lies and abuse appeared) because I was banned from accessing the sites which were carrying the abuse.

Imagine being in a boxing match.

Your opponent can hit you as often and as hard as he likes. He can even hit below the belt. But you aren't allowed to hit back. That's what it was (and is) like.

I tried to find a lawyer to represent me but every lawyer I approached refused to work for me, or to help me find a lawyer who would allow me to give him money. When word got out that I was looking for a libel barrister, one firm of solicitors did offer to give me the name of a barrister specialising in libel if I sent them £1,000. You could feel the smirk in the offer.

The Royal Society of Arts, of which I was a Fellow, expelled me because I was telling the truth and because the BBC had attacked me for telling the truth. That's exactly the same as arresting the victim of a mugging.

'Any honest artist is an agitator, an anarchist, an incendiary.' – George Woodcock

What most people fail to understand is that most social media is controlled by governments, and the bit that isn't controlled by governments is controlled by left wingers who exhibit various stages of megalomania and people who believe that the earth is flat and that Stalin was a good egg.

To begin with, people put my videos and articles onto their YouTube channels and their Twitter accounts. But they soon found that if they do so the material would be removed and, if they continued, they would lose their channels. Material was removed from YouTube channels within ten or fifteen minutes of it appearing.

I was even blocked from appearing on internet radio programmes. When I was interviewed, the station would suddenly stop broadcasting if the interview was live or parts of the interview would mysteriously disappear if it was recorded. Internet radio show hosts who had repeatedly asked me to appear on their programmes suddenly stopped asking. After I appeared on an American podcast, the interviewer told me afterwards that he had lost his Spotify account because he had interviewed me.

In recent years, the demonization has grown to such an extent that I have had huge problems in getting my books published or keeping published books in print.

Publishers stopped publishing existing books which had been around for years, which were still selling well and which had nothing whatsoever to do with covid or climate change.

For example, publishers in Germany and China suddenly abandoned my books, even though they were bestsellers in those countries. One year, my Germany publisher sent me £30,000 in royalties for a couple of books which had been in print for years (the titles were *Bodypower* and *How to Stop Your Doctor Killing You*) and which were regularly selling steadily. And then suddenly those books (and others) disappeared and were no longer available. That cannot possibly have been a purely commercial decision since if an author is making money from his backlist books then the publisher would have also been making a good profit.

In the UK, a major publisher printed but suddenly lost all interest in a book which they had considered exciting. The book appeared without any promotion and the publisher even refused to try to sell paperback rights. I immediately sold the paperback rights myself so it wasn't the book that was unsaleable. Unfortunately, when the first print run of the paperback appeared, the book was not reprinted. That has happened to me several times. One bestselling book sold out before publication but was never reprinted.

Then online publishers refused to publish my books or suddenly withdrew them from sale without giving any reason. Organisations such as PayPal withdrew facilities from another publisher within an hour of their publishing one of my books.

The slow-witted folk who condemn the use of fossil fuels do not seem to realize that fossil fuels have given them the lives they enjoy.

There's all sorts of rubbish about me on the internet these days, some of it egregiously out of context, some of it just lies and most of it emanating from Wikipedia, Google and the other garbage distributors controlled by the conspirators.

Someone in Bangkok went through over 5,000 articles I'd written for the national press (around 10 million words altogether) to find something with which Wikipedia could berate me. All they could come up with was an article about AIDS which I wrote when I was *The Sun* doctor in the 1980s. Unfortunately for them, every word I wrote was absolutely accurate and based on medical journal papers.

The big question is why would anyone in Bangkok bother to spend all that time reading through so many of my old newspaper cuttings?

(The Wikipedia editors, some of whom are possibly linked to the CIA according to one of the site's founders, were so miffed that they couldn't find any errors that they decided to abandon facts and truth and just called me discredited and a conspiracy theorist. They added in the AIDS stuff because they wrongly thought it was a stick with which they could beat me.)

The really odd thing is that in the 80s I was considered an expert on AIDS. I was invited to make a keynote speech at a major conference on AIDS. And I regularly broadcast about AIDS.

But Wikipedia and Google aren't much interested in inconvenient truths.

The Wikipedia page in my name was altered after my first video about the coronavirus hoax.

And, oddly, Wikipedia appears to have sealed my page so that no decent people can do anything to it.

Larry Sanger the co-founder of Wikipedia, who has since denounced the site, reckons that at least one of those involved in removing the truth from my page, and replacing facts with garbage, is linked to the CIA.

That's bad enough, but I have been approached by a Wikipedia editor offering to remove the lies and replace the truths which were removed if I hand over money. To my mind that rather suggests that Wikipedia is nothing but a protection racket. If I hand over the £500 required, another editor will simply put the garbage back. And then the protection racket will continue indefinitely.

What's the difference between this racket and the one where a restaurant owner forks over so much a week for his restaurant not to be attacked?

I regard Wikipedia as a powerful force for evil – because of its links to Google it has probably done more to suppress the truth than any other website. It is worth remembering that most of the people doing stuff for Wikipedia are anonymous amateurs who presumably do what they do to enjoy a sense of power and to feel important and relevant – emotions they never enjoy in their miserable and pathetic real lives. Many entries in what is described as an encyclopaedia are written by teenagers with no qualifications, knowledge or experience.

And some editors, do what they do for 'protection' or 'bribe' money. 'Give us money and Wikipedia will say nice things about you.'

Sadly, Wikipedia is still regarded by some as a reference tool – though in my view it long ago became corrupt and entirely untrustworthy. Today the Wikipedia pages are too often written by spies and liars and read only by the naïve and simple-minded. It is worth noting that Wikipedia publishes a disclaimer on every page (right at the bottom in the sort of small print which tells you that your freezer warranty will expire twenty seconds after you turn on the appliance) which says (in capital letters): 'WIKIPEDIA MAKES

NO GUARANTEE OF VALIDITY'.

Moreover, on the same page, Wikipedia says: 'None of the contributors, sponsors, administrators, or anyone else connected with Wikipedia in any way whatsoever can be responsible for the appearance of any inaccurate or libellous information or for your use of the information contained in or linked from these web pages.'

So, in short, Wikipedia can lie about me, destroy my life and walk away whistling.

And Google (which has a deal with Wikipedia which means that it carries Wikipedia's garbage on its own site) can also walk away whistling.

So, there you are, dear reader. If an 18-year-old Wikipedia editor dislikes you, or picks you out at random, he can describe you as a paedophile and a serial killer and there is nothing you can do about it. Your life will be ruined but you have no recourse

If there is a more disreputable internet site than Wikipedia I have yet to find it.

In addition to re-editing my biography (putting in lies and taking out truths) Wikipedia editors removed a Wikipedia page devoted to my bestselling series of 15 books in *The Young Country Doctor* series. The books, about the residents of the village of Bilbury, are set in the 1970s and have nothing to do with covid since they were mostly written a decade or two ago. I'm told editors also removed the Wikipedia page devoted to my series of four books about Mrs Caldicot. I think they eventually left the page devoted to the film of *Mrs Caldicot's Cabbage War* starring Pauline Collins, John Alderton, Peter Capaldi and company – though I understand that attempts were made to remove that. An editor also described me as a 'conspiracy theorist' on that page.

Why would they do any of this?

None of these books had anything to do with covid-19 or covid jabs.

Was it possibly done out of spite? Or just to damage my reputation still further?

Who knows.

Incidentally, I'm told that my Wikipedia page was edited by someone called Philip Cross.

This is what Larry Sanger (co-founder of Wikipedia) has to say about Philip Cross.

'In public discussion of Wikipedia corruption, among the topics that come up are the CIA and other government agencies editing; the 'Philip Cross' account which cannot be that of a single person; the 'Wiki-PR' company which edited Wikipedia for pay on behalf of many famous and powerful people and companies; and certain of Jimmy Wales' associates, including Tony Blair and officials in Kazakhstan.'

And here is what Larry Sanger says in his book *Essays on Free Knowledge*: 'I believe Wikipedia is thoroughly corrupt – the information in it is carefully massaged through behind-the-scenes control and payoffs.'

In September 2022, I reported that Wikipedia, the encyclopaedia which is edited by amateurs, had been fined $88,000 for publishing information considered to be false. The fine related to 'misinformation'.

Wikipedia has, I believe, single-handedly destroyed the credibility of the internet and degraded the word encyclopaedia.

Larry Sanger has pointed out that the search engine Google (which has itself frequently been fined huge sums) helped establish Wikipedia's 'undeserved popular perception of credibility'. Google, which Sanger reveals has 'contributed millions to Wikipedia', summarises and promotes Wikipedia material as though it were reliable and impartial.

Wikipedia is used to destroy the credibility of people whose work might be inconvenient for the conspirators. The brainless and undiscerning who use Wikipedia often believe they are receiving the definitive view on a subject. This is nonsense, of course. Even when the security services aren't involved, all Wikipedia provides is the one-sided view of a bigot or a clique of bigots. Wikipedia is inadequately researched and poorly written by amateurs, many of whom are incompetent, vindictive, ignorant, bigoted, venal and corrupt. Wikipedia is not a tool; it is, rather, a weapon for control, deceit and demonization and for spreading misinformation. Wikipedia is a danger to freedom. If Wikipedia was genuinely interested in providing honest information, the editors of every page would be publicly named and their qualifications listed. They don't do that because the average Wikipedia editor would turn out to be 15-years-old, have an IQ of 97 and possess no qualifications whatsoever.

The anonymity offered by the internet has allowed cowardly bullies to say whatever they like, and tell whatever lies they fancy, without fear of retribution. The internet in general, and social media in particular, were designed for cowards and bullies. Many of those cowards and bullies have now become Wikipedia editors.

Wikipedia and Google aren't much interested in inconvenient truths. They have, instead, found a simple route to massive wealth. The last time I looked, Alphabet (the new name for Google and YouTube) had 150,000 employees with a median pay of £252,000 a year. That is, to be blunt, obscene and entirely undeserved.

Here's how Wikipedia works.

After I first exposed the covid fraud, I was described as 'discredited' by a solitary Wikipedia editor. There was no evidence whatsoever for this libellous claim. (But Wikipedia stands above the law and refuses to allow itself to be sued for libel.)

A small, local newspaper then duly described me as 'discredited' because they'd pulled the word off Wikipedia.

And a Wikipedia editor (probably the one who had created the libel in the first place) then used the local newspaper story as evidence for the claim – putting the newspaper in its list of references.

Mission accomplished. I had officially become 'discredited'.

The conspirators have been planning their coup for a long, long time. And they have got very good at it. They have pretty well all the money and power in the world. Aided and abetted by collaborating left wing activists (a polite way of saying 'toxic communists') some of whom who have swallowed the poisonous lies, and many of whom are paid to follow the party line, they have taken control and are ruthlessly and relentlessly pushing and pulling us towards the Great Reset.

The English parliament and institutions used to be led (largely, at least) by honest and honourable men and women who cared about their responsibilities. Today, Parliament and the institutions consist of men and women who are devoid of any sense of responsibility. Both are run by greedy, self-serving individuals whose only interest is in furthering their own ambitions. And the medical establishment, all of it, was bought long ago by the pharmaceutical industry and is now full of whores. The only thing that could possibly be said in their favour is that they certainly didn't come cheaply.

Around the world, Britain used to be respected and admired. Today, we are laughed at and our southern shores are thick with self-proclaimed asylum seekers who don't love or admire England but who have come here because we (or rather our leaders) give them money (our money) and ask them no questions.

All of this, the endless deceits, the propaganda and the censorship and the abuse have had other serious effects on our society. One result of the sense of chaos, fear and oppression has been an increase in intolerance, resentment, and shaming as well as the sort of sense of entitlement exemplified by the UK's royal family. And, of course, a lack of a sense of humour.

In a recent survey, half of under 25-year-olds said that some people deserve to be 'cancelled' with many agreeing (with no recorded sense of shame or embarrassment) that they themselves had little or no tolerance for people who had views with which they disagreed.

Young left-wing neoliberals (the new power group in our society since they have a stranglehold on social media) claim to be in favour of human rights and freedom. But they are only in favour of their rights and their freedom, and in that they are closer in spirit to the fascists they pretend to abhor than the liberals they claim to be.

All of this promotes Statism (the very essence of the Great Reset) and diminishes our freedom.

Those who talk about food shortages (because the world's population is too big) should remember that food is now so abundant that in the United States four out of ten white adults are obese. And for black people the figure is five out of ten.

Even today, after much hacking, suppressing, censoring and banning, more people visit my website and watch my videos than watch the BBC's flagship news programme 'Newsnight'.

Back in the middle of April 2022, I wrote an article in which I expressed concern that the conspirators were pushing us into World War. The title of that article was 'Do the Conspirators Now Want World III?'

Well, I suspect that they do.

The journalists and collaborators who sneered and scoffed, and said it could never happen, were clearly wrong – again.

The fraudulent pandemic, the covid-19 jabs, the lockdowns, the masks and the panoply of psychological, brain washing tricks introduced by lying, cheating governments and government advisors, were designed to terrify and to force populations to learn to obey whatever instructions they were given and to accept whatever lies they were told.

The aim, as we knew all along, was to reduce the size of the world's population. That's what the conspirators frequently told us. And that is what they meant.

The covid-19 jab will kill many. Abandoning the elderly, the sick and the disabled will kill millions. The growing famine in Asia and Africa will kill a billion or so. But that won't be fast enough. A good, chronic, designer war will ruin economies and help kill billions.

And it is possible because the conspirators have suppressed the truth, demonised the truth-tellers and terrified millions into becoming collaborators in their evil conspiracy.

Right from the start I felt it was patently clear that what was happening in Ukraine was being used as an excuse to build up enthusiasm for World War III.

And since the beginning of what is best described as an Orwellian designer war, the conspirators have been working hard to push the collaborating public (brains softened by too many months of mask wearing and too many toxic injections) into demanding a war against Russia.

The UK Government – which has debts up to its collective eyeballs – is spending tens of billions a year on sending bullets and bombs to Ukraine to make sure that the war continues and gets worse – including depleted uranium shells and those particularly horrid grenades which are designed to take the arms and legs off inquisitive children. And British and American troops will be in Ukraine.

Putin is being pushed into a corner in the hope that he will become so desperate that he drops nuclear bombs on Ukraine. That's precisely what the conspirators want.

A pitiful melange of morons and cretins, blind to what is happening, their brains frazzled by the toxic covid jab, are screaming their support for Ukraine – without having any idea what is happening or why.

None of them gives a damn for the umpteen other wars in the world (e.g. Yemen and Syria) or for the fact that Ukraine and Russia have long-standing form for squabbling and killing each other's citizens. None of them cares that Ukraine is as guilty of war crimes as Russia.

Brainwashed and ignorant they wave their little Ukraine flags, as mindless and as pathetic as drunken football fans on the rampage. Councils, and concerned but brain dead citizens, fly Ukraine flags on their flagpoles, and purr smugly with self-satisfaction. Motorists have Ukraine flags attached to their cars. People who look intelligent and human have Ukraine badges in their lapels. None of them has the brains to realise that they are merely pawns in an Orwellian game of deceit and control.

In the same way that Germany's invasion of Poland led to World War II, so it is now clear that Russia's invasion of Ukraine could be used as an excuse for the conspirators to start World War III.

As I argued back in April 2022, there is no longer any doubt that NATO deliberately pushed Russia into invading Ukraine. Nor is there any doubt that this is not, by far, the most egregious military activity occurring at the moment. The wars in Yemen and Syria have killed far more people but have aroused little or no interest among Western politicians or journalists.

I don't think anyone who has studied the evidence would disagree with the conclusion that Russia was inspired to invade Ukraine in order to help further the plans of those prosecuting the Great Reset.

The food, fuel and fertiliser shortages which are a direct result of the orchestrated invasion will wreck the global economy and force up inflation, prices and interest rates.

In the West, particularly Europe, there will be much hardship. Millions will lose their jobs and millions will lose their homes.

But the real cost will be felt in Africa and Asia where hundreds of millions will die of starvation in the coming months. It would be naïve to think that this was anything other than deliberate genocide. The politicians responsible for the deadly sanctions against Russia should be treated as war criminals. Those sanctions have done their greatest damage in Western Europe.

The media has done its job well. Letter columns are full of demands for more action, more bullets, more war. Political leaders talk of deposing Putin and arresting him.

The people who have been brainwashed into demanding a greater war have been manipulated and do not realise that they are being used. They are the same people who fell for the recycling myth. They're the people who fell for the global warming myth. They're the people who accepted the toxic, experimental jabs with unfettered enthusiasm. These people have been moulded and trained and turned into gullible, compliant servants of the Great Reset conspiracy.

Individual Russian citizens (who may not have committed any crimes, let alone been involved in the invasion of Ukraine) have been hounded and punished. Sportsmen and musicians who happen to be Russian have been denied the opportunity to ply their trades simply because they carry Russian passports. Businessmen are seeing their property taken from them – simply because of their citizenship. There is talk of confiscating assets from all Russian citizens.

The conspirators who have controlled the world for the last two years, and whose publicly avowed aims include genocide, digital enslavement and a world government have pushed the public into demanding that Britain, America and other countries become even more directly involved in the conflict in Ukraine.

These are bad times, orchestrated and conducted by evil conspirators.

The only certainty is that the conspirators are in control. And the innocent stooges who wear, wave or fly their little flags in support of Ukraine are playing into their hands.

The conspirators created this conflict. And it is becoming increasingly clear that they aren't finished with it.

'Naturally, the common people don't want war; neither in Russia, nor in England, nor for that matter in Germany. That is understood. But, after all, it is the leaders of the country who determine the policy and it is always a simple matter to drag the people along, whether it is a democracy or a fascist dictatorship, or a parliament, or a communist dictatorship. Voice or no voice the people can always be brought to the bidding of the leaders. That is easy. All you have to do is tell them they are being attacked and denounce the peacemakers for lack of patriotism and exposing the country to danger; it works the same in any country.'

The man who said that was Hermann Goering.

Hitler's second in command was speaking before being sentenced to death at the Nuremburg trials.

Our existence is threatened by the unnerving rise of the illiterate.

It is sometimes claimed that social media is a useful weapon against tyranny. But that is clearly not true. Social media is totally controlled and utterly corrupt.

I am not allowed on any social media channels because I have consistently told the truth about covid-19 and covid-19 'vaccination'.

I have never published any inaccurate, frightening or misleading material. I have never published anything illegal or professionally improper. And yet right from the start of 2020 I have been banned from social media. Many of the bans were clearly cruel and vindictive. For example, YouTube has removed old television programmes in which I appeared many years ago. There was absolutely no logical reason for this, and the items were clearly removed simply to try to whitewash me from the internet and remove anything which might have added to my credibility.

For me there is now no free speech.

The personal cost is enormous.

It is usual these days for authors to sell their books by promoting them on social media. I cannot promote my books on any social media sites (and, of course, I am denied all access to the mainstream media). I cannot counter libellous material about me which appears on social media sites. And I cannot question fake sites in my name which have nothing to do with me. (I should mention, again, that I never monetised my videos on YouTube and so never made a penny out of them. Those who claimed I made videos to make money were lying. It's worth noting that some of those with successful YouTube channels are making over £1,000,000 a year. And, of course, other social media sites such as TikTok can be equally profitable.)

Because I am banned and libelled endlessly, publishers will not publish my books and newspapers and magazines will not review them. Printers and publishers who specialise in internet books refuse to publish my work. Several of my books have been published and then withdrawn. Media companies will not allow me to buy advertising. All I can do is publish myself and sell my books on Amazon. (Amazon has banned several of my books. But I should be grateful, and I am, that they allow me to publish most of my self-published books on their platform.)

The war we are fighting has, since the beginning, been a one-sided war because the enemy has always controlled all of the mainstream media and much of the internet. We have been fighting with our eyes blindfolded and with both arms tied behind our backs. The surprise is that we continue to succeed in worrying the oppressors who are so determined to hide the truth.

It has become increasingly clear in recent years that social media has resulted in the polarisation of views. Even where debate is (theoretically) allowed, there is no debate. The young (in particular) have no inclination to debate their views, and do not have the skills to argue in support of their beliefs. And so, instead of debate, we have a 'cancel culture', which is simply a new phrase referring to censorship. Those who adopt an outlandish and indefensible view point ('there are no germs', 'the earth is flat', 'a biological male can become a biological female simply by wanting to change', 'there is no gravity', 'climate change is a real threat' and so on) refuse to discuss their views, or to provide any real evidence for them, but instead simply brand their opponents as awful, hateful, dangerous and so on, and respond with threats and attempts to destroy the individual and their career.

Since this is the policy which has been adopted by governments in the last few years (in refusing to allow any debate at all about the value, effectiveness and safety of vaccination, for example) it is difficult to avoid the conclusion that 'cancel culture' is a deliberate policy of the conspirators, which has promoted this notion because it serves their malignant ends.

Antoinette and I have had to deal with a number of prejudiced and bigoted people since I was lied about and labelled a discredited conspiracy theorist.

So, for example, a local chemist (a branch of a chain called Lloyds since you ask) suddenly found it impossible to obtain the tamoxifen which Antoinette has to take as a daily treatment for her breast cancer. However, one quick email showed that the wholesaler the chemist used had the drug in stock. (We managed to find another chemist who obtained the drug the next day).

And a roofer who had agreed to mend our broken roof, found out about my views on covid-19 and suddenly decided that he wouldn't help us after all.

Early in 2020, I pointed out that governments everywhere had been using a range of Orwellian mind control tricks during the coronavirus 'crisis'. The slogans, the clapping and the symbols had all been carefully used to enable the authorities to take control of our thinking.

Dr Colin Barron, a former NHS doctor and eminent hypnotherapist who is the author of the book *Practical Hypnotherapy*, pointed out to me just how our minds had been taken over and how we had been very successfully and skilfully manipulated into believing the lies we had been fed.

Elected governments, aided by specialist behavioural scientists, used trickery to brainwash millions into accepting the coronavirus propaganda.

The mind is a wonderful thing. It responds in sometimes unpredictable ways. So, for example, if you see a headline which says: 'Boris Johnson is an alien' then most people will probably dismiss it quite readily. But if the headline says 'Is Boris Johnson an alien?' readers will be more likely to suspect that the former British Prime Minister might indeed be from another planet. And research shows that if people see a headline which says, 'Boris Johnson is NOT an alien' then their suspicions will be raised still higher.

Manipulating and tricking the mind is a professional business.

The mass of people have been quietly hypnotised and indoctrinated to accept the new mass hysteria generated by governments everywhere.

Do you remember who said: 'Through clever and constant application of propaganda people can be made to see paradise as hell and also the other way round, to consider the most wretched life as paradise.'?

It was Adolf Hitler, who was a master at mass manipulation and the use of subliminal techniques.

And it was Hitler who also commented that it was good fortune for governments that the mass of people did not think.

The Nazis were very good at controlling people's minds.

Goebbels, who was Hitler's propaganda chief, once said that if you repeat a lie often enough then people will believe it. He also pointed out that if you want to control a population and you have to deal with opposition then you should accuse the other side of the sin or the trickery which you yourself are using.

So, governments everywhere have been accusing those who are telling the truth of spreading fake news. Anyone who doesn't toe the party line is dismissed as a dangerous conspiracy theorist – though the big conspiracies have all been coming from governments.

Countries around the world promoted slogans to persuade their citizens to behave as required. In China there was a slogan which said 'If you love your parents, lock them up'. In Taiwan people were told: 'To visit each other is to kill each other'.

At first glance the slogans which were heavily advertised in the UK seemed harmless enough.

The first trio of phrases which were promoted everywhere were:

Keep your distance, Wash your hands, Think of others

Then other new phrases were added to the repertoire:

Stay home, Save lives, Protect the NHS

The rhythm and pattern used in these phrases is not a coincidence. There are usually three words in each phrase and the phrases run in threes.

As Dr Colin Barron explained to me, using phrases of three words, presented in groups of three, is a technique known as the rule of three in psychological conditioning.

And that's the reason for the three phrases with which we are all being bombarded. We've being trained and taught at the same time. It's behavioural psychology.

Other hypnotherapists have pointed out that if we repeat phrases often enough then the words and thoughts become implanted in our subconscious minds and then become a belief which motivates our behaviour. And so governments repeat slogans which become beliefs. It's called auto suggestion – along the lines of 'every day in every way I am getting better and better'.

Hitler was also a believer that if a lie was repeated often enough it would eventually be confused with the truth by the greater part of the population.

'People more readily fall victim to the big lie than the small lie,' said Hitler, 'since it would never come into their heads to fabricate colossal untruths, and they would not believe that others could have the impudence to distort the truth so infamously.'

Hitler used these techniques to control and manipulate the German people and to persuade them to accept the evil things he wanted them to do.

George Orwell who invented Newspeak, also understood the importance of the triple three word phrase. In 1984, his futuristic novel which was written in 1948, Orwell invented the slogan: 'War is peace, Freedom is slavery, Ignorance is strength'.

If you want a picture of the future, wrote Orwell, imagine a boot stamping on a human face – for ever. Power, he reminded us, is not a means, it is an end.

Everything that has happened since February 2020 is part of the brainwashing process.

The instructions we were given were more like orders. The signs that popped up like dandelions said 'Stand here' not 'Please stand here'.

You don't say 'Please' to prisoners do you?

And then there were the weeks of clapping for carers and medical staff.

Telling people to stand on their doorsteps at 8 p.m. on Thursdays and to clap was a simple, repetitive task – part of the mass hypnosis. The clapping may have started out innocently but it was quickly and enthusiastically promoted by the people influencing our lives.

Persuading people to do what you want them to do is part of the hypnotherapy process. Getting people to clap was also important in that it made people believe in the danger of the coronavirus and the bravery of those working in health care. It helped people accept the fact that there were no beds available for patients with cancer or any other disorder.

The rainbow which suddenly started to appear everywhere was another part of the brainwashing process.

Even the confusing rules about who we could and could not see were part of the programme. A minister told Britons that two people could meet one person but that one person could not meet two people. An obvious contradictory nonsense.

If you confuse and bewilder at the same time that you are frightening people then you unsettle them and create an anxious and obedient population.

Bearing all this in mind I prepared my own triple phrased slogan. Three words and three phrases:

Distrust the government; Avoid mass media; Fight the lies

My slogans fit the brainwashing requirement perfectly: simple, effective, honest.

We cannot be silenced.

If I have to find a soap box or stand on street corners handing out hand written leaflets then that's what I will do.

We have built this society. It is our responsibility. If we stay silent then the evil will be done with our blessing.

Here is the transcript of a video of mine which was called 'Coronavirus: Why Did YouTube Ban My Video?' The video appeared on the 13th May 2020.

'I was shocked but not surprised when YouTube took down one of my videos recently.

I was shocked because everything I said in the video was absolutely accurate and honest. The only conceivable problem was that the video didn't follow the authorised line being heavily promoted by governments all over the world.

A huge number of doctors now agree with me that governments have made huge mistakes in the way they have dealt with this virus. I've been saying this since February. Their propaganda has created much fear and I don't think anyone in government now denies that the number of people dying because of the lockdowns – the so-called 'cure' for the coronavirus – will be far, far greater than the number who will die from the virus itself. Governments everywhere have distorted truths and misled their populations.

My only aim has always been to provide some truths and, hopefully, some reassurance. I have never allowed advertising or sponsorship on my videos or my website. Both exist as what used to be called a public service. I don't make TV or radio programmes and I don't write articles or columns any more. Everything I've written or recorded about the coronavirus has resulted in my reputation being trashed so much that I would have been far better off if I'd kept my thoughts to myself.

I've never been able to do the sensible thing. My life has been one of fighting for lost and difficult causes and truths. I've spent most of my many years battling for people and animals without enough care for the consequences. And I'm pretty used to being banned and lied about, sneered at and patronised.

I said I was shocked but not surprised by YouTube's decision.

I wasn't surprised because YouTube seems to have got itself an unfortunate reputation for censoring people who put up videos on its channel.

Well, it's their channel. They are the publishers. So they can, if they like, allow only State approved lobbyists to put up videos.

But if anyone from YouTube ever bothers to watch this before deciding to ban it, because it doesn't follow the official party line, I've got a thought for you.

Some years ago I resigned from a well-paid column on a British Sunday newspaper because the editor refused to print a column questioning the validity of the Iraq War. I didn't believe in the weapons of mass destruction claims and I thought we were being lied to. I didn't see the point in writing a column if I wasn't allowed to express my honestly felt views. Resigning from that column on a matter of principle meant that I didn't get any more newspaper work. Editors don't much like columnists who have principles – and it cost me dearly in financial terms.

But that newspaper has been slowly dying since then.

The circulation fell by around 90% in the years which followed. Now, you could argue that the circulation fell that much because I resigned and I wouldn't stop you if you did but I wouldn't really believe it. And you could argue that the circulation fell because all newspapers are losing circulation and that's true. But this particular newspaper has lost a devil of a lot more circulation than it should have done.

And I think I know why.

It is slowly dying because it lost its integrity. It doesn't stand for anything. It didn't respect its readers. And the readers saw or sensed that lack of respect.

In a way it's tricky being a publisher.

If you're going to retain your integrity and ensure that your readers or viewers know that you respect their intelligence then you have to put up with people wanting to write or say things you don't agree with.

When the men and women in suits tell you to ban this or censor that you have to have the guts to say 'No' or someone else with more integrity will come along and put you out of business.

You obviously have to censor people who tell blatant lies or want to publish dangerous or illegal material. But you can't suppress the truth and expect to retain respect and goodwill. Leaving people alone to tell the truth or share their opinions needs courage and basic integrity. You have to recognise that you cannot have freedom without a free press. Remember those newspaper editors in old cowboy movies? They always had courage to print the truth.

It was HL Mencken who wrote that the relationship of a journalist to a politician should be that of a dog to a lamppost. And it was Theodore Roosevelt who, to paraphrase slightly, wrote that thinking there must be no criticism of the establishment is not only unpatriotic and servile but morally treasonable.

It seems to me that the people at YouTube don't have either integrity or courage. More importantly they don't realise that the heart and soul of any publishing company belongs to the readers.

The video of mine which YouTube took down contained nothing but the truth. I've been researching and writing medical matters for a long time – a lot longer than YouTube has been in existence. I'm not stupid. I'm not going to write or say something I think is wrong.

Why did they try to censor me?

They could, I suppose, be like those terrible students who want to ban anyone who says something they don't like. But I don't think that's it. That wouldn't make commercial sense.

Maybe they just prefer to follow the safe route and specialise in publishing videos of ducks on roller skates.

But I don't think that's it. That wouldn't make commercial sense either.

Or, maybe they just disapprove of original thinking that doesn't fit neatly into government approved propaganda.

I was banned in China years ago so I know how that works. Statist, fascist, establishment organisations have been doing it for a long time.

I think YouTube has been got at. I don't think it's YouTube anymore. I think it's ThemTube.

I think they're suppressing material which the authorities don't want publishing. I think that the men and women in suits have convinced them that anyone who questions authority is a mad, dangerous conspiracy theorist. Well look at my track record – it's all listed on my website. I'm not mad and I'm not a conspiracy theorist – though I suppose that if you're a fascist dictator I might be considered dangerous.

This time it's a lot easier for me than when I resigned as a columnist and prior to that when I resigned as a GP because I didn't approve of what the Government was doing.

So, I don't really care what YouTube decides to do.

If they want to restore a little of that lost integrity they could put back the videos they banned.

But if the sycophants at YouTube ban me completely I really don't give a fig.

I was banned and suppressed long before YouTube appeared – long before the internet appeared.

Once before when I was banned I wrote that I would, if necessary, write out my articles and hand them out on street corners. Or sell my books from a wheelbarrow. And I still mean that.

If they do remove this or any of my other videos then everyone who cares about freedom and free speech will know that YouTube is no more than a worthless propaganda vessel – specialising in indoctrination.

The script of this video is going onto my website and I hope everyone who can do so will put the tape in places where YouTube can't remove it. I'm banned from Facebook and so on because I'm considered a threat. It's the modern day version of book burning.

So put this tape on your Facebook page or Twitter or whatever.

Or put a link to my website so that people can read the truth directly. Tell everyone to watch or listen or to read my website. It's all free. No ads. No sponsors. No one ever tells me what to write or what not to write.

Stand up for the truth. It's really quite important.'

Note: You will not be surprised to know that YouTube quickly removed this video from their platform. Those who put the video or the transcript onto their social media pages had their social media pages temporarily removed.

People are sometimes surprised when I tell them that YouTube has banned me from watching other people's videos. I then usually send them the message I received from YouTube. I could, I suspect, get round the ban by finding an internet café and using another name and computer but I wouldn't want to enter the house of someone who didn't want me as a guest and I don't want to have anything to do with YouTube which is, in my view, an utter disgrace. I wish people would boycott it (or at least stop making videos for the platform) but sadly I know that's not going to happen. However, it is worth remembering that every time someone watches a video on YouTube, the result is that YouTube gets richer, stronger and more powerful.

In September 2023 I found it interesting to see that the *New York Post* (and other media organisations) questioned the way that Russell Brand was attacked in the media and had his YouTube channel demonetised after he had been accused of sexual offences including rape. 'Are accusations enough to destroy someone's life and remove his ability to make money?' asks the *Post*. The argument, with which I agree, is that a man or woman should be regarded as innocent until proven guilty.

Well, try this for size. I haven't been accused of anything. But for the crime of telling the truth about covid (and no one has found any errors in over 300 videos and several million words on my websites) I have been destroyed and lied about and falsely labelled a discredited conspiracy theorist. As a result of simply telling the truth I have lost agents and publishers who produced my books in 26 languages and most countries in the world. All gone. I've also been banned from all mainstream media, all social media and most of the internet. My YouTube channel (never monetised) was completely removed and I was banned from accessing other people's YouTube videos. And when I moved to BrandNewTube that platform was destroyed.

But no one in the media found my bans worth reporting.

This article (and the video that went with it) first appeared early in 2020. The revelation about the BBC's self-imposed censorship is still vitally important.

'The pro vaxxers, as I call them, deny that vaccines can cause problems, even though governments have paid out billions of dollars of taxpayers' money in compensation to previously healthy people who were made ill or killed by vaccines.

In the UK, the NHS helpfully lists the side effects which might occur with the flu vaccine. They say that flu vaccines are very safe and the side effects they list are muscle aches, a slightly raised temperature and a sore arm where the needle went in. They do say that very rarely individuals may have an anaphylactic shock reaction, though they forget to mention that this can kill you. And don't worry, they say, the people who vaccinate you will be trained to deal with allergic reactions. Oh yes? It won't be just a junior nurse or care assistant, then? Or a soldier? Or the AA man?

I didn't see nausea and headaches though they are listed on the CDC site in America.

Oddly, the NHS also seems to say that none of the flu vaccines contains live viruses so they cannot give you flu. They worry a lot about that, the pro-vaxxers.

There are incidentally very few or no anti-vaxxers, though the drug company spokespersons like to pretend there are.

There are, on the one hand, people like me, who like to examine medical issues according to the facts and there are the pro-vaxxers who accept what the drug companies tell them. A good number of pro-vaxxers are closely linked to the drug industry and not a few receive money from it. The rest are just woefully ignorant simpletons.

By drug industry, by the way, I am referring not to the dealers who market Columbian marching powder but to the international companies which make legal prescription drugs – which are responsible for far, far more addicts, illnesses and deaths.

We should, of course, remember that the nasal vaccine, the one given to children, contains attenuated or weakened live viruses.

It is possible that if a child has a weakened immune system – as might be the case if they'd been imprisoned and kept indoors a lot or had for absolutely no good reason been wearing a mask for a long time – then a vaccine virus might conceivably cause the flu.

And because attenuated viruses aren't quite dead they could change or even become live and they could mutate and they could result in other people being infected. So it is possible that if a child has the nasal flu vaccine they could transmit the flu virus to Granny – who might die as a result. That's the sort of warning governments like to give these days so I thought I ought to follow their example.

I have dealt with the nasal flu vaccine in a previous video but at the moment I am more interested in the injected vaccine because the NHS's official list of flu vaccine side effects, as presented to reassure patients, seems a bit on the skimpy side to me.

So here, in contrast, is the official list of side effects for one flu vaccine. This list is intended for the use of health professionals. Some of these side effects will be commoner than others, of course. But if you get a side effect then it doesn't matter if it's common or not.

If I had wanted to be sly, in a politician sort of way, I could perhaps have found the side effects from half a dozen flu vaccines – and since the lists wouldn't have been the same I would have had a longer list. But I'm not a politician. So, here is the list of some of the possible side effects with just one flu vaccine taken at random. I've made my list alphabetical since that's a reasonably traditional and fair thing to do. It's obviously, therefore, not something the BBC would consider.

Allergy reactions including anaphylactic shock which can kill of course, so that's not one you want because it would be a real disappointment to be perfectly healthy, have a flu jab and then die. I've had an anaphylactic shock reaction and it was no fun at all. Not recommended. No one really knows how common it is but it's a fair guess that several hundred people a year have them as a result of vaccination.

Arthralgia – pain in your joints
Asthenia – a lack of energy and weakness
Convulsions – definitely not something you want
Diarrhoea – messy but probably won't kill you
Ecchymosis – a bruise
Encephalomyelitis – inflammation of the brain and spinal cord, you don't want that one
Erythema Multiforme
Fatigue
Fever
Guillain-Barre Syndrome – which can cause paralysis, so that's one to avoid
Headache
Induration – hardening
Influenza type illness
Malaise
Myalgia – pain in your muscles
Nausea
Neuralgia
Neuritis
Pain
Parasthesia
Pruritis
Rash
Redness
Shivering
Sweating
Swelling
Syncope – loss of consciousness, not a lot of fun if you're a

steeplejack, bus driver or almost anything
Tenderness at injection site
Thrombocytopenia – that's a blood disorder which you definitely
don't want.
Urticaria
Vasculitis which may be associated with transient renal involvement
– renal of course is kidneys so that's not a good one to have
and
Vomiting – which like diarrhoea can be very messy

Those are the side effects listed being associated with one particular
flu vaccine. But I'm not allowed to tell you about those because the
list is only really available for health professionals who are
considered better able to deal with them. So I shouldn't have told
you about those side effects. So forget I did or I'll probably be in
trouble. Again.

Oh, and of course, this list isn't complete because it is always
possible that additional problems may develop a year or more later.
And some side effects, particularly rare ones, may not be recorded –
even if they are deadly.

And the upside of the flu vaccine?

Well, there is a chance that the vaccine may lower your chances
of getting the flu.

No guarantee, of course.

Some flu jabs don't work terribly well at all.

In a good year the vaccine can reduce your risk of needing to see
the doctor with the flu by between 40 and 60 per cent. In other years
the effectiveness is much lower than that. That's the truth according
to the CDC in America. The flu vaccine can sometimes be effective
in just 14% of patients. So six out of seven patients take all those
risks for absolutely no benefit.

But the pro-vaxxers, who find truth rather uncomfortable and not
quite to their taste it seems to me, may forget to tell you any of that.

A lot of pro-vaxxers aren't very good at science and are pretty
crappy when it comes to facts.

And now, here is a confession for which I am grateful to Richie
Allen, the host of the Richie Allen Radio Show.

On 23rd September, on a BBC programme called Radio Five
Live, which I confess I've never listened to and which probably has

three listeners, someone called Emma Barnett said something quite extraordinary.

'We actually don't, as a matter of editorial policy, we don't debate with anti-vaxxers, whether they're right or wrong. We actually don't do that.'

Staggering.

Note Ms Barnett's words – 'right or wrong'.

Only if you had never done any research could you think that this policy is a good one. The world of vaccination can really only be divided into two groups: the pro-vaxxers, who are blind to the truth and keen to suppress it because it is inconvenient or uncomfortable, and the truth seekers who are open minded and who possess scientific curiosity.

Boris Johnson has described us truth seekers as nuts, and since that comes from a man who has proved himself to me to be an imbecile in that he appears to have deliberately rejected the real scientific evidence, a traitor in that he appears to have betrayed the people he is paid to look after and Britain's first self-appointed dictator that can probably be regarded as a compliment.

I've never heard of this Emma, indeed the only Emma I was previously aware of was Emma Hamilton who was the mistress of Lord Nelson and who died in 1815 though I don't suppose being dead would prevent her having a job with the BBC. Indeed, it might be considered an advantage.

What qualifications do you need for a job like this?

O level arrogance? Ability to make a nice cup of tea?

Where do they find people prepared to take a job with these strictures? Do they import them, give them a bag of chips and point them at a microphone? I have no idea.

Anyway, that's what young Emma had to say about the BBC's attitude towards the truth about vaccines on the BBC. I'm quoting it because no one except *Guardian* readers and Bill and Melinda Gates, listen to anything on the BBC – it's a cultural backwater which has been stagnant for decades.

So there we are.

The BBC – paid for with our money, well not actually mine because I don't give them any – seems to be deliberately and openly suppressing the scientific truths about vaccines. Emma almost seems sort of proud of it. 'We don't do that.' She talks about it as though she's talking about not spitting on the pavement or shoplifting or passing wind in public. It's as though she feels the corporation's prejudice and anti-scientific approach gives her the right to assume the high moral ground.

The fear, of course, is that many people may die as a result of the BBC policy.

If the pro-vaxx argument goes unquestioned then problems may never be solved. Thousands of people are seriously and often permanently injured because vaccines are not properly tested or because drug companies hide evidence. I wonder if little Emma understands what transverse myelitis involves? Or how parents feel when a perfectly healthy child has a vaccination which leaves them permanently brain damaged. One life lost and two lives permanently scarred. I wonder if she understands that governments promote vaccination for economic reasons not health reasons. Does she have any idea how much vaccine companies cheat and lie?

This policy of a blanket ban on those who question vaccination means that anyone who fights for the truth will be dismissed not as truth seekers but as anti-vaxxers.

To me Emma seems utterly hubristic and, at the same time, shamelessly pathetic. And the organisation employing her is worse. There is an arrogance, an assumption at the BBC that the people who question vaccination, and who argue that there are risks which may exceed the benefits, are lunatics. They seem to believe that the science has been sorted in favour of vaccination. But that is wrong and narrow-minded.

My first book, which was published in 1975, was called *The Medicine Men* and it was about the way the damage the drug industry often does – and the way it has bought, literally bought, huge parts of the medical establishment. The BBC thought *The Medicine Men* was so important that they gave the book a 15 to 20 minute segment on their main news programme. *The Guardian* newspaper serialised the book. That was in the 1970s.

My how things change.

How did the BBC suddenly know better than the science? Who told them that vaccines are so good that there is no need to debate their value, their safety or their effectiveness? I bet you there's a drug company lurking somewhere.

I don't think Whitty, Vallance and Hancock will debate with me in the UK, even though I have written extensively about these things for decades, because they know they will look foolish. I can prove that vaccines kill and injure and often don't work at all.

The BBC's unjustifiable arrogance rather explains why the BBC, despite constantly harassing me to pay their licence fee so that they can add it to the loot from Bill Gates, won't now invite me to discuss vaccination on any of its programmes.

But why won't the BBC bosses allow criticism of vaccination on its airwaves?

Could it possibly be because the BBC knows damned well that any moderately competent doctor who knows the scientific truths about vaccine safety and ineffectiveness could utterly destroy the BBC's stale, cosy and entirely fake pro-vax argument live on air?

Could it be that the bean counters at the BBC are frightened that this might upset the BBC's cosy relationship with arch pro-vaxxers the Bill and Melinda Gates Foundation?

And why do staff such as Emma Barnett allow this to happen? Whatever happened to editorial integrity and independence?

Have BBC staff sold their integrity and honour for big fat salaries, perhaps? Is this why BBC staff tend to be very highly paid? Is it vanity? Get your picture in the *Radio Times* and a chance to sidle up and get Gary Lineker's autograph in the staff canteen?

Half asleep, I could shred the pro-vax arguments and leave them beyond repair.

I'm not what the BBC would call an anti-vaxxer but I can prove that some of the companies making vaccines have been found guilty of fraud and bribery. I can prove that billions of dollars have been paid out in compensation to people injured by vaccines.

But maybe little Emma and her colleagues aren't interested in any of those uncomfortable truths which relate to real people, science and death.

I think that decent broadcasters would walk away from an organisation which has such oppressive policies – out of tune with an obligation to the public. The BBC is a propaganda department for, among others, the powerful, rich and fraudulent vaccine industry.

Did they cover the importance of morality and ethics when you studied broadcasting, Emma?

Why does the BBC feel the need to have such outrageous

prejudices?

Who makes up the BBC's biased, prejudiced and bigoted policies? The Bill and Melinda Gates Foundation perhaps?

What an utter disgrace this organisation is. It exists to educate and inform the public. It is surely supposed to be fair and unbiased. Lord Reith would weep.

Many BBC presenters probably doesn't know who the hell he was. But he'd weep. He'd weep. He is identified with the BBC's aims to educate, inform and entertain.

In my view if you deliberately suppress scientific truths that would be inconvenient to one of your financial partners then you deserve all the opprobrium that is available.

You may have heard that one of the volunteers in the AstraZeneca trial for a covid-19 vaccine suffered from transverse myelitis – a rare and potentially serious disease that can cause paralysis.

Well, now a second volunteer has allegedly fallen ill. Apparently another case of transverse myelitis.

This isn't all that surprising.

That's two serious problems in just 18,000 volunteers. So far.

The British authorities apparently allowed trials to continue but trials were stopped in the US. And AstraZeneca is reputed to be already making billions of doses of its rubbish. Sorry its vaccine.

But wait!

Stop the presses.

AstraZeneca says in an internal document that the two cases were 'unlikely to be associated with the vaccine, or there was insufficient evidence to say for certain that the illnesses were or were not related to the vaccine.'

So, according to AstraZeneca, it is just an unlucky coincidence that two of their guinea pigs happened to develop exactly the same rare disease at almost exactly the same time.

That was handy because the halt in the trial had resulted in the share price of AstraZeneca falling by 11.3 billion dollars.

And although the pro-vaxxers insist that this was all just a coincidence, the fact is that transverse myelitis is one of the top vaccine injuries for which patients receive compensation. The total at the moment, in the USA, is apparently around $150 million in damages. That's just for transverse myelitis. And it is a nasty disease. The symptoms can include pain, muscle weakness, bladder and bowel problems and paralysis. Tragically, two thirds of those who have transverse myelitis remain permanently damaged.

Apart from apparently being very unlucky, what sort of company is Astra Zeneca?

The BBC wouldn't let me on their airwaves to tell you this but in 2014, Astra Zeneca agreed to pay $110 million to settle two lawsuits brought by the state of Texas, claiming that it had fraudulently marketed two drugs. AstraZeneca has paid out hundreds of millions of dollars to resolve thousands of lawsuits and it has been charged with illegal marketing, including corrupt data in studies for marketing a drug to children, a sex scandal and a poorly run clinical trial that could have compromised patient safety and data reliability.

Studies which showed that a drug produced harmful results were never published and were covered up. A company email revealed: 'Thus far, we have buried trials 15,31,56. The larger issue is how do we face the outside world when they begin to criticise us for suppressing data.' After years of investigations, Astra Zeneca paid a $520 million fine in the US and paid $647 million to settle global lawsuits.

These are the people the Government and the BBC want us to trust.

Could the BBC be legally responsible when people who have been denied the truth, fall ill? Surely the BBC has a legal responsibility to provide both sides of a scientific discussion with a voice?

The WHO, the private health office of the Bill and Melinda Gates Foundation, says AstraZeneca is the leading candidate for the billions in profit that lie ahead.

So, that's alright then.

Oh, and other drug companies are, as I warned they would be, playing around with a DNA/RNA flu vaccine.

But somehow I doubt if you will hear about the dangers of that on the BBC which doesn't seem to give a stuff for the health of the British public.

Please viewers, I beg you, do not ever give the BBC a penny of your money again. They've been losing listeners and viewers for years – don't do anything illegal but let's speed up the demise of the BBC.

The BBC is a self-confessed biased organisation and I don't think it is a stretch to describe it as corrupt.

Why do I say that?

Well, the BBC refuses to allow presenters to discuss the downside of vaccination. It is deliberately and knowingly refusing to allow any debate on an issue which affects the health, and possibly life, of everyone.

And the BBC has financial links with the world's arch pro-vaxxers – the Bill and Melinda Gates Foundation.

Corruption is fraudulent conduct by those in power – often involving money.

So you decide:

The BBC deliberately and cold-bloodedly suppresses the truth about vaccines (because the pro-vaxxers aren't going to tell you about the dangers) and has financial links with people promoting vaccines.

Is that corruption?

The sooner we get rid of the BBC the safer and healthier we will all be.

If you believe that the BBC is corrupt then anyone who gives money to the BBC is surely guilty of supporting and funding corrupt activities. People who support criminals can be charged. Why can't the BBC and its staff be charged?

Please make sure everyone you know – and even those you don't know – watches this video with the clip of little Emma letting the cat out of the bag. The whoopsie of the year, perchance, and congratulations to my friend Richie Allen for catching it on his machine.

Send a copy of this video to your MP and demand that he or she votes to defund this terrible organisation. Send copies to everyone at the BBC who tweets or who has a Facebook account. Swamp the self-satisfied, smug bastards with some simple truths.

And send leaflets on vaccination – based on the lists on my website – to every politician, every BBC presenter and every pro-vaxxer.

Remember: anyone who is a pro-vaxxer is an ignorant, deluded and dangerous fool.

Oh, and that's not all.

There's one more little scandal that I doubt if young Emma, her colleagues and the prejudiced oafs at the BBC would want to trouble you with.

For months I have been pointing out that Patrick Vallance, Britain's Chief Scientific Advisor, used to work for GlaxoSmithKline – a huge drug company which is in the running to make a vaccine for which, I am told, it is planning to charge the EU around 10 euros a pop.

If they got the deal for all 7 billion people on the planet, that would be 70 billion euros. And, of course, some want us all to have vaccines every three months so that's 280 billion euros a year forever.

And then there will probably be another 280 billion euros for flu vaccines. And, oh boy, soon you're talking real money and Bill Gates will be frothing at the mouth in anticipation.

By the way, you can read all about GlaxoSmithKline on my website. What a company. In medical terms they are what we call a steaming pile of the stuff you get out of the exhaust pipe of a horse.

There's material for information leaflets on www.vernoncoleman.com

I said previously that I would be very surprised if Vallance didn't still have financial links to GSK.

Well, guess what – he does.

Vallance, the British Government's Chief Scientific Adviser is reported to have £600,000 worth of shares in GSK – a big vaccine manufacturer.

And no one in the British Government, or indeed Her Majesty's Opposition, if indeed there still is one somewhere, seems to think that this is wrong though to me is seems very iffy. I'd be upset if I found that an adviser in the Ministry of Defence had shares in a particular tank or bomb manufacturer. Or if a local council planning officer had links with a particular builder. But perhaps I'm just a bit old-fashioned about these things. Old-fashioned values don't seem to be much prized in public life these days.

How much longer are we going to put up with this? We can win this war but we have to take the attack to the traitors.'

You will not be surprised to know that this video was speedily and permanently removed from YouTube.

Free speech is today only available to those who say what they are told to say, or repeat what they expected to say, and who confine their remarks to topics and views with which the establishment do not find uncomfortable.

And anyone who thinks that is free speech is lost to the world.

So much of my work has been stolen, and made available on other people's websites and in their books, that on numerous occasions I have been prevented from reusing my own material because I have lost control of my copyright. There is at least one shameless 'author' on Amazon whose books consist solely of material which he has stolen from me. He isn't a plagiarist. He is a thief.

The plan is to digitalise everything and control everything we do through social credit programmes as have already been introduced in China. They intend to force us to use apps on smart phones because these enable them to keep a close eye on our movements and our activities. Everything we do will be tracked and traced. If they claim that this is for your benefit then they are lying. (I described the essence and horror of social credit in my book 'Social Credit: Nightmare on Your Street'.)

This is not the first time that the media has been bought. But it is the first time that all the media has been bought for a long period.

Right from the start (way back in the 1960s) it was clear that the conspirators had to buy two significant groups if their plan was to succeed. They had to control the media and they had to control the medical profession. It has been said that every great cause begins as a movement, becomes a business and degenerates into a racket. The global warming scam missed out the first two stages and has always been what it is now: a racket.

The medical establishment had to be bought in order to sustain the myth that the world was suffering from a pandemic. Ignorant and compliant members of the medical establishment were brought on board when they were convinced by the scientific nonsense that the climate change threat was a real one. The medical profession as a whole was offered unprecedented bribes in the form of massive, bigger than ever fees for giving covid-19 jabs. It was as simple as that: doctors around the world were bought. And doctors who tried to tell the truth were demonised and had their licences taken away. (Most of the doctors who spoke out were osteopaths and chiropractors who were not liable to have their medical licences taken away because they didn't have medical licences in the first place.)

The same thing happened with the media. Newspapers, magazines and broadcasters around the world were all bought with massive advertising expenditure. Journalists wrote what they were told to write and became public relations people; ignoring truths and promoting the official lies in a way never seen before. And individuals, particularly Bill Gates, the amateur vaccine enthusiast and friend of Jeffrey Epstein, spent hundreds of millions of dollars in buying the allegiance of media groups and of individual journalists. For example, Gates used the money he had made from Microsoft to set up financial arrangements with *The Guardian* newspaper and the BBC in England. The BBC, a once respected publicly funded operation, is in my view the world's leading specialist in providing misinformation and disinformation on all its various channels and outlets. It was the BBC which, with an outrageous disregard for the truth or for public safety, broadcast an item telling the public that there are absolutely no side effects with the covid-19 jab.

It always seemed to me that the conspiracy would only be successful if the conspirators could enlist the media and the health professionals. Those two groups would, in turn, recruit an army of collaborators.

Once journalists and doctors had been bought, the conspirators were able to push forward their plan. (The clampdown on journalists was extraordinary. Journalists I had known for years suddenly refused to talk to me – and wouldn't tell me why.)

The thing to remember about both propaganda and censorship is that most of both are hidden, very well hidden. You may see a few signs but both propaganda and censorship are like icebergs – mostly hidden out of sight. Only when you start to look, and to ask questions, will you see what has happened. My aim in writing this book is to help expose some of the propaganda and some of the censorship but, more importantly, to enable you to spot examples for yourself and to see how you are being manipulated.

Since the beginning of 2020, everything has been entirely predictable. And things have been steadily getting worse. Many commentators and observers who are not members of the conspiracy and not awake to what is happening are bewildered by the chaos and the speed at which things are changing. They frequently admit that they do not know what is happening. They should be aware that in medicine, doctors are trained to try to find a single diagnosis to explain a whole range of symptoms and signs. Once that same diagnostic principle is applied to the way the world is changing, it becomes clear that everything is linked. There is no chaos. The changes which are taking place are all part of a wider agenda. There is one explanation for everything that is happening. We are victims of a global conspiracy.

There is no longer any such thing as justice in the world but the conspirators cannot eradicate the difference between right and wrong.

In George Orwell's book *1984*, the people of Oceana are kept obedient by being constantly reminded that their country is at war. No one knows quite who the opponents are and the war is everlasting. The perpetual state of national emergency enables Big Brother to remove all civil liberties and to introduce travel restrictions, identity cards and countless new laws. Democracy, freedom and human rights are all abolished in the name of patriotism. Censorship and propaganda replace them. Press freedom is abolished because of the threat to national security. Big Brother uses fear (of attack) and hatred (of the unseen enemy) to control citizens who are told that the only way they can preserve their freedom is to give it up.

'It is wiser to find out, than to suppose.' – Mark Twain

'Question with boldness even the existence of God; because if there be one He must approve of the homage of reason more than that of blindfolded fear.' – Thomas Jefferson

It is important to remember that the globalists and the collaborators have weaponised fear. They deliberately created terrifying situations so that they could control the public, enforce compliance and introduce horrendously controlling new regulations.

One drug company spokesperson was quoted as having described mRNA vaccines as 'hacking the software of life and installing a new operating system'.

I don't know about you but I'd prefer to stick with the operating system I was given by God.

I have learned many things in the last twelve months but the one thing I've learned for certain is that there are far more lob dotterels, joltheads and lobcocks around than I would have thought possible.

Politicians, journalists, doctors, celebrity jab drummers and millions of so-called ordinary folk, all think that drug companies are wonderful and can always be trusted.

But how do the vaccine enthusiasts know that the covid jab is safe?

Well, unless they've all been hiding their lights under bushels and doing original research, I assume that their information comes from several sources: the Government, the media, the drug companies and the medical profession.

I have, during the last few months, been astonished at the way politicians and journalists have feted the vaccine-producing drug companies and their executives.

I strongly suspect that solar panels won't work properly in the future.

Activists have for some time been filling the sky with toxic minerals which, they say, will help block the sun's rays. These minerals are what make the sky perennially hazy.

So how will the solar panels work?

If they ever give out gold medals for irony then this phenomenon deserves a mention

Some critics assume that drug companies suddenly became 'crooked' and 'dishonest' with the production of the covid-19 'vaccines'. But that's not true. I first exposed the drug companies in my book *The Medicine Men* which was published nearly half a century ago – in 1975. Drug company staff have been deceitful, misleading and dangerous for decades. Drug industry staffers haven't just got bad. The industry has been institutionally corrupt and devious for many, many years. Employees always take the credit if they produce something useful but never own the blame when things go wrong – as they so often do.

In the early 1970s I applied for a job with a drug company so that I could expose some of the industry's dirty secrets. The company gave me a job but then recognised my name and insisted that I sign a contract promising not to write about anything I discovered. Naturally I declined to sign the contract!

Nevertheless, I still managed to do a good deal of research and to write my book exposing the industry. The book was called *The Medicine Men*.

Days after I wrote *The Medicine Men* a major drug company offered to give me money to go on a speaking tour. The aim, it was clear, to buy me with a considerable pay-off. I laughed at them and said 'No'! (*The Medicine Men* has been republished and is now available again.)

I've been exposing the drug companies ever since.

Here are just some of the ways in which drug companies cheat and put patients' lives at risk:

Drug companies suppress research which they regard as commercially inconvenient. If a research project shows that a new drug is dangerous then the drug company responsible for the research will refuse to publish the results. The truth will 'out' eventually, of course. But by then many thousands of people may have died or been injured.

Drug companies never do research which might highlight serious problems with their products. So, for example, I don't believe vaccine makers do sufficient research to find out if their products are safe for long-term use or safe to be given with other products as part of a mass vaccination programme. I believe there is a desperate need for more research into how vaccines affect the immune system. (My book *Anyone who tells you vaccines are safe and effective is lying* contains some surprising facts. Despite many attempts to destroy the book it is still available. Every newspaper and magazine refused to review it when the book was published.)

Drug companies have bought and corrupted the medical establishment with gifts, money and free holidays. The corruption is so extensive that it is nigh on impossible to find any eminent medical body that isn't stuffed with people who are receiving or have received money from drug companies.

Drug companies use animal experiments to 'prove' that their products are safe for human use. But this is fraudulent. Drug companies know that tests done on animals are unreliable and cannot be trusted. Moreover, tests on animals are recognised as being utterly useless by the industry, the medical profession and the watchdogs. My book *Betrayal of Trust* (now republished) contains details of 50 drugs which caused cancer and other serious problems when given to animals but which were passed for human use. I took a fifteen foot long computer print-out to a House of Commons committee – the print-out contained nothing but the names of drugs which kill animals but are prescribed for people. I wanted the House of Commons to stop experiments on animals. Nothing happened.

Drug companies do everything they can to suppress the truth. When I was hired to speak to NHS staff about drug side effects, drug company bosses forced the company to fire me before I could speak. I was replaced with a drug company employee! When I edited the *British Clinical Journal*, a drug company executive told the publisher to fire me. (He did.) *The European Medical Journal* (which I founded, edited, paid for and ran entirely without drug company advertising) had to close after an expensive lawsuit and injunction paid for by a pro-vivisection pressure group funded by drug companies. The opposing lawyers had more cuttings about me than I had ever seen. They also had copies of private letters which I found a little startling. (I ended up being threatened with a possible prison sentence but managed to save the book publishing imprint EMJ Books out of the wreckage.)

Drug companies control most big charities. They give the charities huge amounts of money to promote their products.

Drug companies pay huge amounts of money for advertising space in medical journals. I don't know of any medical journals which are free of what I see as a significant conflict of interest. I have never accepted advertising on my own books, articles or videos so that there can never be any doubt about my independence.

Drug companies hide or lie about the side effects of drugs – sometimes managing to do this for years.

Drug companies pressurise journalists and editors not to publish critical material. After I wrote a series of articles which a drug company didn't like my research file mysteriously disappeared from a filing cabinet. The editor refused to continue to publish the series because my research file had gone. Drug company pressure spreads far and wide. After I was invited to speak to the Oxford Union in a debate about vivisection the invitation was withdrawn because no drug company employed vivisectionist would speak against me. The vivisectionists were frightened they'd lose the debate and so the Union cancelled me. Drug company lobbyists have helped get my books banned around the world.

Drug companies have a massive amount of influence over statutory bodies which are supposed to protect the public.

Anyone who knows anything about the world's major drug

companies would be less enthusiastic about taking their word on anything.

So, for example, in the UK, Pfizer was fined £84.2 million for overcharging the NHS by 2,600% and in the US Pfizer was hit with a $2.3 billion fine for mis-promoting medicines and paying kickbacks to doctors.

In 2014, AstraZeneca agreed to pay $110 million to settle two lawsuits brought by the state of Texas, claiming that it had fraudulently marketed two drugs. The Texas Attorney General, when he announced the settlements, said the company's alleged actions were 'especially disturbing because the well-being of children and the integrity of the state hospital system were jeopardised'.

AstraZeneca said it denied any wrong doing. So it paid out $110million for not doing anything wrong which was generous.

That wasn't the only little problem for AstraZeneca.

The company had to pay $350 million to resolve 23,000 lawsuits.

The company was also charged with illegal marketing, including corrupt data in studies for marketing a drug to children, a sex scandal and a poorly run clinical trial that could have compromised patient safety and data reliability.

The study for this drug was financed by AstraZeneca and originally included 30 children – that's not particularly small for a drug trial by the way – but only eight children completed the trial and the researcher who conducted the trial concluded that it was inconclusive. The researcher was paid at least $238,000 in consulting fees and travel costs.

However, the study was published anyway and led to a national recommendation that the drug be used as the leading choice for children.

Other studies which showed that a drug produced harmful results were never published and were covered up. A company email revealed: 'Thus far, we have buried trials 15,31,56. The larger issue is how do we face the outside world when they begin to criticise us for suppressing data.'

After years of investigations AstraZeneca paid a $520 million fine in the US and paid $647 million to settle global lawsuits.

In 2014, there was another scandal. After a trial described as sloppy, which resulted in a third of the participants dropping out because of side effects, results published in the *American Journal of*

Psychiatry showed the drug as a 'promising treatment'.

Then, there is GlaxoSmithKline, known to its enemies as GSK.

GSK is one of the world's biggest pharmaceutical companies and in my view if it made toasters you'd never buy a toaster from them.

In 2014, for example, GSK was fined $490 million dollars by China after a Chinese court found it guilty of bribery.

The court gave GSK's former head of Chinese operations a suspended prison sentence and they gave suspended prison sentences to other executives too.

In 2006, GSK paid out $160 million for claims made by patients who had become addicts.

In 2009, GSK paid out $2.5 million to the family of a three-year-old born with severe heart malformations. And in Canada, a five-year-old girl died five days after an H1N1 flu shot and her parents sued GSK for $4.2 million. The parents' lawyer alleged that the drug was brought out quickly and without proper testing as the federal government exerted intense pressure on Canadians to get immunised.

In 2010, GSK paid out $1.14 billion because of claims over a drug called Paxil. And they settled lawsuits over a drug called Avandia for $500 million.

In 2011, GSK paid $250 million to settle 5,500 death and injury claims and set aside $6.4 billion for future lawsuits and settlements in respect of the drug Avandia.

In 2016, GSK paid out $6.2 million in Canada.

In 2017, GSK were ordered to pay $3 million to a widow.

In 2018, GSK faced 445 lawsuits over a drug called Zofran.

In 2012, GSK pleaded guilty to federal criminal offences including misbranding of two antidepressants and failure to report safety data about a drug for diabetes to the FDA in America. The company admitted to illegally promoting Paxil for the treatment of depression in children and agreed to pay a fine of $3 billion. That was the largest health care fraud settlement in US history. GSK also reached a related civil settlement with the US Justice Department. The $3 billion fine also included the civil penalties for improper marketing of half a dozen other drugs.

GSK is one of the top earning vaccine companies in the world. And in 2010, there were reports of narcolepsy occurring in Sweden and Finland among children who had the H1N1 swine flu vaccine. It is reported that not all the safety problems were made public. I have seen a report that by December 2009, for each one million doses of the vaccine given about 76 cases of serious adverse events were reported though this was not made public. A paper published in the British medical Journal in 2018 reported that GSK had commented that `further research is needed to confirm what role Pandemrix may have played in the development of narcolepsy among those involved.'

The writer of the BMJ article commented: `Now, eight years after the outbreak, new information is emerging from one of the lawsuits that, months before the narcolepsy cases were reported the manufacturer and public health officials were aware of other serious adverse events logged in relation to Pandemrix. '

Sir Patrick Vallance, who was the Chief Scientific Adviser in the United Kingdom during the fake pandemic, and, I suspect, a key figure in dealing with the coronavirus in the UK, worked for GSK between 2006 and 2018. By the time he left GSK he was a member of the board and the corporate executive team. All of the fines and so on which I have listed took place while Vallance was working as a senior figure at GSK.

Drug company Johnson and Johnson has been linked with clinical trials in new-born babies, infants and pregnant women. I truly find it difficult to believe this is happening. Still, no doubt the BBC and the rest of the rotten media will be enthusiastic and forget to mention that J&J had to set aside $3.9 billion after lawsuits related to it flogging baby powder contaminated with asbestos.

And then there was $8 billion in punitive damages in 2019 after the company failed to warn that one of its drugs could lead to breast growth in boys. And $2.2 billion in civil and criminal fines for the same drug. And a huge multi million judgement after the company played a part in the opiod crisis.

Have you noticed how many amazing coincidences there are these days? Thousands of people die shortly after having the covid-19 jab and they're all put down as death by coincidence.

There's a pandemic of coincidences.

Individuals cannot sue covid-19 vaccine manufacturers if anything goes wrong.

And the Medicines Health Regulatory Authority and Public Health England both agree with the UK Government and insist that there haven't been any adverse events worth noting with the covid jabs.

I'm not surprised. Both organisations have received huge sums of money from the Bill and Melinda Gates Foundation which had huge shareholdings in vaccine manufacturers.

Bill and Melinda will no doubt be delighted to hear that Pfizer expects to generate $15 billion, or a quarter of its total revenue, from sales of its covid-19 jab. Moreover Pfizer say they expect there to be a long lasting need for covid-19 injections to combat new variants and boost waning immune responses.

The Bill and Melinda Gates Foundation also had financial links to Moderna, of course. And that should lead to more profits. The company was reported to believe that sales would reach almost $19 billion in 2021. (In 2019, pre-covid, Moderna made a loss.)

The power of the drug companies is everywhere. When the *Spectator* magazine ran what it calls 'a Health Summit to examine the priorities of the NHS' the small print informed potential attendees that: 'The event is in association with AbbVie and Eli Lilly and Company and is funded by both organisations.'

That seemed to me to be like hiring the Yorkshire Ripper to help fund a symposium on safety for prostitutes.

I think the *Spectator* should be ashamed. But I doubt if they will be. Money talks with a loud voice.

Eli Lilly is an American drug company which in 2009 pleaded guilty to illegally marketing a drug called Zyprexa. The company paid a $1.4 billion fine which included a criminal fine. AbbVie is a biopharmaceutical company. In July 2022, the company agreed to pay $2.37 billion to settle lawsuits over the marketing of opioid painkillers. (The company was accused of deceptive marketing practices.)

For the record, I regard it as an honour that drug companies seem to regard me as their No 1 Enemy.

Some people probably think I am unfair to drug companies. Consider the following facts.

The last time I was sued by drug companies, a bunch of them got together and hired flashy lawyers and process servers. The court papers were so extensive that they wouldn't fit through the letter box and the bailiff had to push them through the cat flap. I discovered that the drug companies' lawyer had far more press cuttings about me than I had ever seen. They even had copies of private letters.

When I was working as a magazine editor, the publisher had a meeting with a drug company boss. 'How do I get you to advertise in the magazine?' asked the publisher. 'Sack him!' said the drug company boss, pointing at me. I was duly sacked.

The pressure didn't always come from drug companies. I was sacked from TV AM (where I was the TV AM doctor) after I talked about the health dangers of dairy produce. The station received letters threatening to pull advertising. The station did wait a couple of weeks before deciding that I was no longer required.

I was invited to be a main speaker, about drug side effects, to a large conference of senior doctors, senior nurses and administrators – all working for the NHS. When the drug industry complained about my presence in the conference the organisers dumped me. They hired someone from the drug industry to speak in my place.

Throughout the 1970s, 1980s and 1990s I wrote an average of five weekly columns. Drug companies regularly complained to editors whenever I wrote about vaccination, vivisection and drug side effects. Some editors ignored the complaints. But some didn't. Drug company hacks (paid by drug companies) would regularly offer to write free weekly columns so that editors would fire me and run the free columns. Fortunately, it didn't usually work because the free columns were patronising and dull.

I have more experience of drug company deceits than anyone and I would rather trust one of the Columbian drug barons than a drug company employee.

Doctors writing in the *British Medical Journal* have called for the medical profession to do less screening of patients and to cut back on prescribing treatment – 'to help combat climate change'. Doctors called for global warming concerns to be put above patients' interests.

Let's get this straight: the medical establishment wants to cut back on diagnosing cancer early in order to save Big Ben from disappearing under 100 foot waves a week on Wednesday.

This is terrifyingly wicked.

'The climate emergency is the true health crisis of our time,' is the message from the medical establishment. Doctors' leaders appear to have had their brains removed and replaced with those of 12-year-olds. The members of the medical establishment who believe this should all be certified insane and put into a coma to protect the public from their deranged utterings.

The nonsense from the BMA is pouring out these days.

For example, the BMA now says that Britain needs another 60,000 doctors.

Britain doesn't need any more doctors. Dare I suggest that the NHS needs the GPs on the payroll to do what they're paid for – which is to see patients? The Department of Health in the UK has reported that the average GP is now working a three day week and earning over £100,000.

Doctors protest that they are overworked and that they are struggling to deal with a continuing crisis. But GPs are working three day weeks! It's no wonder patients are more likely to win the lottery than get an appointment with their doctor. When I last practised medicine, GPs visited their patients at weekends and nights and if a patient couldn't make their way to the surgery then the doctor visited them at home. Today, a large number of GPs won't ever see patients in the flesh and certainly won't lower themselves to take blood samples, syringe ears or remove stitches. The unfortunate patient in need of one of these services has to make another appointment to see a nurse, health care assistant or, quite possibly, the practice cleaner. It may sound strange but I think GPs lost their way when they stopped syringing wax out of blocked ears.

Today, the medical profession is complicit in the Government's attack on the people it is paid to serve.

The Government repeatedly agrees with the BMA's claims that Britain desperately needs more doctors.

But if the Government really wants to increase the number of GPs, it should invite retired GPs to emerge from retirement – and perhaps work part-time. (After all, many existing, younger GPs only work two or three days a week to reduce their tax liabilities. And that's part of the reason for the shortage. Older GPs working half a week each would improve the health service considerably.)

But this won't happen.

The Government does not want older, experienced, independent-minded doctors working in Britain.

It is difficult to avoid the thought, by the way, that the GMC's absurd revalidation programme was deliberately introduced to force older, experienced, independent doctors out of the medical profession – thereby making it easier to destroy the NHS, to kill vast numbers of elderly and sick patients and to push through the rebranded flu hoax and the associated fraud involving an experimental injection.

Maybe the Government realised that older, more experienced doctors, not bound by an NHS contract, without mortgages to pay and without future careers to worry about, might be more likely to question the whole rebranded flu hoax. It is noteworthy that most of the few doctors objecting to the fraud have been older and more experienced physicians.

According to a report in the London *Sunday Times*, the *British Medical Association* is being transformed by a hard-line group of doctors led by an anonymous steering committee, which has seized power. (It is surprising how many anonymous power brokers there are now in the world. I am not even allowed to access social media sites but from the little I have seen I suspect that the greatest influence comes from individuals who are anonymous.)

It is the hardliner BMA members who are leading the strikes which are resulting in thousands of cancer patients dying before their treatment can even start.

It is now commonplace for patients who are seeking emergency help to have to wait 24 hours in an accident and emergency department before they are seen – and even then they may be seen by a nurse or a student rather than a qualified doctor. The pressure on accident and emergency departments has risen dramatically since GPs stopped seeing patients outside office hours. And for a GP, remember, office hours now usually consist of a two or three day working week.

Doctors used to be independent. Sadly, they have now become slaves to a powerful system run by the medical establishment and controlled by the pharmaceutical industry.

Today, doctors are happily leading us into the Great Reset.

I first warned about the unhealthy relationship between doctors and the pharmaceutical industry in my book *The Medicine Men* which was first published in1975.

Doctors have, I regret to say, proved themselves to be as caring and as honourable as estate agents.

The following article appeared on my website on 28th July 2023:

'I recently received a copy of a statement made by Mr Philip Banfield, a doctor who is the BMA UK Council Chair and who spoke at the official covid inquiry.

Banfield said: 'Speaking in my capacity as BMA chair of council, I was acutely aware of the responsibility I held not only of speaking on behalf of its association and all its members, but for every single doctor working in our health service and the millions of patients they care for.'

I didn't know whether to cry, scream or punch the wall when I read that. The arrogance! Banfield was not speaking for all doctors.

And he certainly was not speaking for patients. The BMA has been the patients' enemy for years, and never more than it is now. BMA strikes are causing untold damage to endless numbers of patients. Not surprisingly, hospital and GP patients are increasingly dissatisfied with the care they receive. For Banfield to claim that he was speaking for patients is simply extraordinary and shows a level of disconnect that I find deeply worrying.

If BMA members had the guts to strike for better health care, for an end to working practices which have led to the longest waiting times in history or for the end of the General Medical Council's absurd disciplinary process which punishes doctors who dare to ask questions or share truths, then I would not approve of their methods (doctors are never entitled to withdraw their labour by going on strike) but I would approve of their motives.

But BMA members are striking for more money.

Consultants on an average salary of £128,000 (plus pension and assorted extra payments) are striking for an above inflation pay rise. They must know they cannot possibly receive such a pay rise. If they did they would destroy what is left of the National Health Service and they would help push inflation still higher. Junior doctors (who can earn over £60,000 a year) want a 35% pay rise. They're as likely to get that as I am to be interviewed by the BBC.

The doctors' strikes are official BMA strikes. Far from caring for patients, the BMA appears be using them as a weapon, boasting recently that one in six people will soon be on waiting lists if doctors don't receive the 35% pay rise they are demanding.

It is the BMA which has, in my view, helped destroy health care in the UK. It was the decision of GPs not to work nights or weekends which destroyed hospitals and the ambulance service. And today the average GP works around three days a week. Librarians and accountants work longer hours than GPs.

Does the BMA want to destroy health care in Britain? Or does it want to destroy Britain?

I'm pretty sure it's the latter. It seems to me that the BMA is helping to take us into a world of 15 minute cities, digitalisation, mass vaccination programmes and the Great Reset. It was, I remember, the BMA which said that climate change should be a new priority for doctors. It seems to concern them not at all that climate change is just a myth – and a myth, like covid and vaccination which must never, ever be debated.

Banfield of the BMA went on to discuss covid-19 as though it were a real pandemic. Did he really not know that the evidence proves that covid-19 was no more than the rebranded flu? Does he really not know that doctors and hospitals and bureaucrats and politicians killed more people than covid-19? Does he not know that all scientific debate was crushed by the medical establishment? Does he not know that the covid-19 'vaccine' does not do what it is supposed to do and is so toxic that it should not have been given to one patient – let alone billions?

If he doesn't know these things it may be because the medical establishment of which he is a part has crushed all debate and helped silence those telling the truth.

Once again I issue my now well-worn challenge.

I challenge Mr Banfield to debate his so-called pandemic, live on national television. I will prove to him that everything the medical establishment did made things worse. Those BMA members who followed the official party line and who wore masks and gave covid jabs were behaving like ignorant fools. They were the problem – not the solution. They should be ashamed.

But Mr Banfield won't accept my challenge, of course. Even if he wanted to he wouldn't be allowed to risk it. The establishment dare not risk allowing the truth to be broadcast on mainstream media.

And they know that I'd chew up Mr Banfield and spit him out in bits because I have the truth on my side. I can prove very quickly that if one of us is speaking on behalf of patients it isn't him.'

There was, of course, no reply to the challenge.

In June 2020, I reported on my websites that a journalist had complained that writing about the coronavirus in Tanzania was dangerous because the Government there was silencing the media.

This was reported in the British mainstream media as though it were a terrible example of censorship and the oppression of the truth.

Most of my remaining laughs have withered a little in recent months but I managed one for this for I think those who appeared to be shocked by this story need to look a little closer to home, and open their eyes.

There has been no freedom of speech anywhere in the world for a long time.

Anyone who questions the 'official' line, which appears to be that the coronavirus which causes covid-19 is a deadly killer which threatens the very existence of the human race, is ignored while every incident or even suggestion which might be used as ammunition to scare people is promoted with hysterical enthusiasm.

To those of us who care about facts the BBC, which receives money from many sources, including some given directly from the Government, the EU and, inevitably, the Gates Foundation, is a particular nightmare.

There is a Woman's Hour programme on the wireless but the State broadcaster would have a collective fit if anyone suggested a programme entitled Man's Hour. There is a Radio Scotland, a Radio Wales and two stations in Northern Ireland but no Radio England. I suspect that is because Scotland, Wales and Northern Ireland are recognised as regions by the European Union but the EU demanded that England be divided into a number of smaller regions.

Despite its charter and national responsibility, the BBC has always been biased and corrupt but it has travelled further along that road than I ever thought possible. Not content with gouging huge licence fees from the British public the BBC seems to be happy to accept money from anyone who wants to buy its favours. I have reported before on the massive multi-million payments which have been paid to the BBC by the European Union but many will have been shocked to hear that the BBC also happily pockets huge sums from a wide variety of associates including the Bill and Melinda Gates Foundation. (It is, of course, a coincidence that Bill Gates appears to be revered by the BBC which always seems to describe anything slightly critical of Gates as 'fake news' or 'false claims'.)

We shouldn't forget that the BBC has been using news as a weapon of war for a long time. Goebbels said in 1944 that the British 'know that news can be a weapon and are experts in its strategy'. And it was the BBC which the Government used as the gun.

George Orwell is said to have learned about Newspeak and Doublespeak while working for the BBC and some suspect that his Ministry of Truth in the book *1984* was modelled on the BBC building in Portland Place.

In 1953, the BBC was used to spearhead the British propaganda campaign in Iran which led to the elected government being toppled.

And the BBC has a long tradition of blacklisting and denouncing critics. They have perhaps just lost a little of the subtlety in recent years.

Orwell knew, as do all proper writers, that it is a writer's job to stand up for victims, to protect the vulnerable and to oppose oppression. I am appalled that the mass market media has betrayed the people and that just about all the columnists active at the moment seem content to follow the party line. I feel able to offer criticism since I resigned from my last Fleet Street column some years ago when the editor of the newspaper I was working for refused to print a column criticising the Iraq War and Tony Blair's lies about the weapons of destruction.

As a writer I am disgusted by the way journalists have taken the knee to their editors and proprietors in order to please the Government. It is a journalist's job to behave like dogs and to treat politicians like lampposts.

And as a former GP I am appalled at the way the science has been distorted and rearranged to suit dishonest motives.

The tests which were widely used for covid-19 turned out to be appalling unreliable but governments persisted in using them.

At the very beginning of the fraud, I urged governments to do more testing – to find out how many people had, or had had, the bug. It seemed sensible. But they steadfastly refused to do this – finding new reasons or excuses on an almost daily basis.

But once they knew they had an unsuitable and unreliable test they made it available very widely in order to find more people with the disease and, therefore, introduce more lockdowns.

Governments claimed that having the disease made individuals a menace to society. With each infected individual a sort of Typhoid Mary of our times. And so if there were enough people in one area testing positive they could shut down everyone and everything as a punishment and, mainly, as a message to everyone else.

The conspirators have done everything possible to oppress us and make life more difficult. The conspirators' yearning for a cashless society is becoming more blatant by the day. I have been warning about this for several decades. People used to laugh at my fears. They don't laugh quite so much now.

In March 2020, in the UK alone, 1,250 free to use cash machines were converted to charge a fee when people take their own money out of the bank. And you have to use a machine because banks are too terrified of the plague to deal with mundane activities such as providing their customers with some of their own money over the counter.

No one seems to care that one in five Britons, and the figures are much the same everywhere, cannot cope without cash because they don't have or don't trust plastic, have poor broadband or mobile phone coverage or are frightened of debt. People don't get into uncontrollable debt using cash. But they do get into uncontrollable debt using credit cards.

Of course cash carries bugs. It always has. So just wash your hands after using it.

A broadcaster working for the BBC has called for big cities to ban any overtaking of cycles by cars and has suggested (also apparently earnestly, though with the BBC that is not always easy to assume) that drivers of motor cars should pull over and allow cyclists to pass if they see them in their rear view mirror.

I feel deeply sorry for anyone under 60 and particularly for those who have small children or grandchildren. If we cannot stop this savage attempt to drive us into the New Abnormal, or the Global Reset promoted by the unelected and self-appointed rulers who have decided that the world is theirs and who are determined to control our lives, there will be little future for any of us.

Everywhere we look there is manipulation of one sort or another.

Newspapers and television cannot do anything without sponsorship of one kind or another. I'm proud that my videos and my remaining website are free of advertising and sponsorship.

The motto for the new media paradigm is (or should be): Censorship, Deception and Misinformation. As in: 'When you think Mainstream Media think Censorship, Deception and Misinformation' or, more specifically: 'When you think of the BBC think Censorship, Deception and Misinformation'.

As I explained in my book *Their Terrifying Plan*, we live in dark, difficult and dangerous times.

The drive towards the Great Reset is continuing apace and I fear that there is little we can do now to prevent the conspirators and the collaborators from their plans.

One aim, of course, is to stop us travelling so that we use less oil. (The stuff is running out and the conspirators want to preserve what there is for themselves.) And the changes to our world are happening every day and are affecting everything we do.

When I was a boy and then a student, my love for the game of cricket grew during the summer holidays in August. Because I had no school and no homework I could spend wonderful days at cricket grounds.

In the summer of 2023 there was no English first class cricket in the month of August.

None.

'A democracy cannot exist as a permanent form of government. It can only exist until the majority discovers it can vote itself largesse out of the public treasury. After that, the majority always votes for the candidate promising the most benefits with the result that democracy collapses because of the loose fiscal policy ensuing, always to be followed by a dictatorship, then a monarchy.' – Alexander Fraser Tytler (1747-1813)

How many people know that Dr Jonas Salk, famous for his polio vaccine, was also the author of a book entitled *The Survival of the Wisest*.

I read the whole thing so that you don't have to and I doubt if it would have been published at all if the author hadn't had something of a reputation as a scientist.

Here is a sample section: 'If human life is to express as much harmony, constructiveness and creativity as are possible for fulfilling the purpose of life, as 'required' by Nature, and the purposes in life, as 'chosen' by Man, attitude will be needed, not of Man 'against' Nature, but of Man 'inclusive with' Nature. A more reasonable attitude would be for Man to 'serve himself' without regard for, or at the expense of, Nature and others.'

Hmm. Clarity was perhaps not Dr Salk's main talent.

In 1973 he also wrote: "Mutations' as here defined, would also be produced by the introduction, either naturally or experimentally, of a virus into a sperm or egg cell, the genetic information of which would then be incorporated in either the DNA or the RNA and transmitted. Such new information might be advantageous or disadvantageous. Nevertheless, it would be transmitted hereditarily, having become part of the organism, whose survival value would then be tested in the process of natural selection.'

And now you can sit up and start to ponder.

Our society is built on trash. A third of what we throw away is less than a year old. The average Briton throws away 72 items of clothing a year. And only a tenth of the old clothes donated to charity shops are suitable to sell in their outlets. The rest are so poorly made or so dirty that they are sent overseas, usually to countries which don't want them. Countries which have tried to stop the flow of rubbish have found themselves on the wrong end of American trade sanctions.

Those who attack truth-telling book authors invariably sniff and sneer at self-published work. They say that because it has not been published by a smart publishing house then a book cannot have any value. I seem to have been particularly targeted by critics. What they don't bother to notice, of course, is that in the past my books have been published in the UK by well-known paperbackers such as Penguin, Pan, Corgi, Arrow and so on and by hardback publishers such as Macmillan, Sidgwick and Jackson and Thames and Hudson. Around the world my books have been published by scores of the world's leading publishers.

And the award winning film *Mrs Caldicot's Cabbage War* was based on my self-published novel of the same name.

The problem is, of course, that mainstream publishers will not publish anything critical of the establishment and so those of us wanting to write books which criticise the Great Reset, the pharmaceutical industry and the medical establishment now have no choice but to self-publish.

A surprisingly large number of people frown on self-published books. I wonder if those scornful, snobbish folk realise that authors who have published books which they have written themselves include Beatrix Potter, Walter Scott, J.M. Barrie, Lewis Carroll, Charles Dickens, T.S.Elliot, Virginia Woolf, Enid Blyton and Mark Twain.

And on the subject of books, reviewers sometimes say lovely things about my books, and for this I am very grateful. But, inevitably, there are many people who (either because they are paid to do so or because they feel strongly that they are right and I am wrong) will give a book a damaging one star review without bothering to buy or read a copy. My books are littered with examples of this – though most of those giving one star reviews prefer not to leave any comment (and therefore do not identify themselves in any way).

In addition to researching and writing about drug treatment, iatrogenesis and drug side effects, I have been writing about the power of the human body to defend itself for well over 50 years – with enthusiasm. Back in the 1970s and 1980s, I wrote hundreds of thousands of words about the power and self-repairing capabilities of the human body in remaining healthy and resisting disease – both in dozens of articles and in books which sold around the world and introduced the concept to millions. I have continued to write about these principles (and, in particular, the way in which the human body can protect and heal itself) in many of my books. I think I am entitled to say, therefore, that, unlike those who hurl abuse at me, and who decorate their abuse with extraordinary flashes of ignorance, I know of what I speak.

So, here are some indisputable facts:

Those who do not believe in germ theory seem uncertain as to the parameters of their argument. Some talk about germs and some specify viruses. Some say there are no infectious diseases. And some say that the human body has no immune system. The less well educated (who seem prolific in their writings, usually prefer to remain anonymous and display a breath-taking mixture of arrogance and ignorance) really do need to understand that not all germs are viruses – there are also bacteria for example. Since the most commonly expressed theory seems to be that there are no germs, let's stick with that for the moment.

Like most people I have known about the germ theory since nearly everyone in my primary school class caught chickenpox at the same time. More confirmatory evidence was provided weekly when I was a GP and saw numerous infectious diseases spread through families and communities.

Those who claim that there are no infectious diseases should take a look a little more at the science of epidemiology. As a starting point I recommend the excellent work of Dr Pickles who practised in

Yorkshire, England in the 20th century. He was a GP but his ground-breaking work on the spread of infections was of vital importance. No one can claim to understand germ theory without a proper understanding of the science of epidemiology and once you understand epidemiology it is impossible not to accept germ theory. The science and principles of epidemiology stand upon germ theory as writing stands upon the alphabet.

Those who would like to dismiss germ theory completely must first explain away Dr John Snow's success in ridding an area of London of cholera, simply by removing the Broad Street pump handle. This, of course, is quite impossible unless you accept germ theory. Before the fake pandemic started, Snow was widely regarded within the medical profession as the most significant medical thinker of all time. You cannot begin to understand the significance of infectious disease in medical practice without reading *The Case Books of Dr John Snow*. Also, how do those who would dismiss germ theory explain the spread of smallpox among Native American Indians when they were given infected blankets by the Spanish?

Those who dismiss the germ theory are replete with opinions, assertions, misinterpretations, extrapolations and anecdotes but not much in the way of science. Shouting and hurling abuse are not evidence but are, rather, a meaningless distraction from more vital issues. Attempts to argue against germ theory are impossible to sustain in scientific terms and are rather akin to trying to argue that the earth is flat. (I have noted that many of those who claim that germs do not exist also claim that the earth is flat. I suspect that this is not a coincidence.) All my working life I have told readers to question everything they read or hear (including everything I've written or said, of course). But healthy scepticism does not mean automatically rejecting everything that has been proved to be true.

The controversy over the germ theory has been adopted by fifth columnists and controlled opposition. These are frequently bullies and are responsible for much of the abuse and arrant pseudoscientific nonsense appearing online. Their plan is a simple one: to make the truth-tellers look stupid to the rest of the world by claiming that germs and infections don't exist – and to annoy those of us who have been telling the truth since the start of this conspiracy. I fear that anyone who complains about these words will, wittingly or unwittingly, be representing the conspiracy.

I wonder how many of those who claim there are no germs would be willing to have a surgical operation without the surgeon washing his hands or wearing gloves. In Victorian times (pre-Lister) surgeons would operate in their street clothes and sharpen their knives on the soles of their boots. Most of the patients who were subjected to surgical procedures under these conditions died from infections contracted on the operating table. Do those who don't believe in germs really believe that patients died or survived by coincidence? Lister proved the significance of germs in the operating theatre beyond any question. His work was vital.

I strongly urge those who do not believe in the existence of germs to study the observations and experience of Dr Ignaz Semmelweis. They will find his experiences instructive. If there is no germ theory then Semmelweis was wrong and Semmelweis cannot have been wrong because his actions, in putting his theory into practice and dramatically reducing the incidence of puerperal fever in the hospital where he worked, proved that he was right. All women who go safely through childbirth owe Semmelweis a big thank you. The history of medicine is packed with similar stories which are ignored as simply 'inconvenient' by those who foolishly claim that there are no germs and no infections.

In February 2020 when I first questioned the covid threat on my website and argued that the so-called coronavirus threat was no more than the annual flu rebranded, I was immediately attacked by the conspirators' handmaidens. However, I have proved time and time again (using government statistics) that covid-19 is merely the rebranded flu. Even the WHO admitted that when covid-19 appeared the traditional flu disappeared. And the figures show that the number of deaths caused by covid-19 matched the number of deaths from the flu in previous years. Covid-19 was nothing more nor less than the annual flu but it was deliberately marketed to create fear and provide an excuse to introduce a toxic vaccine.

Most of the rather hysterical, sometimes simple-minded and often abusive converts who promote the idea that there are no germs (some claim that there are no viruses but this is merely a variation on an unsustainable, pseudoscientific theme) have no medical training or practical experience and their belief is, I suspect, balanced on the very dubious notion that everything we have been taught is a lie.

I suspect that most don't realise that they are being used by the conspirators who are intent on pushing us towards the Great Reset.

Why do I say this?

Well, for a start, many of those who promote the idea that there are no germs still have channels on YouTube. The conspirators don't want them removed because promoting the idea that germs don't exist suits their purpose very well in that it is such a stupid notion that it makes the truth-telling movement a laughing stock to the greater world.

For over half a century now I have earned my living doing research and dispelling propaganda, lies and deceits – wherever their origin was.

I have worked as a hospital doctor and a GP principal and I have edited two medical journals and written papers for many more. I founded and edited my own medical journal which eventually had to close after an expensive legal action brought by a syndicate of drug companies. I never accepted any advertising for my journal – which I had to subsidise with my book earnings. I've also written scores of papers for numerous medical and scientific journals.

But, like most truth-tellers, my YouTube channel was, of course, removed in its entirety. And YouTube went back years to remove TV programmes and appearances I'd made decades ago.

Whatever reputation I had before I was monstered and vilified by Google et al, was built on one simple fact: I told the truth about vaccines, drugs and scandalously over-promoted diseases such as AIDS and covid-19. Many years ago I was the first doctor to point out that doctors were one of the top three causes of death and illness – alongside cancer and circulatory disorders.

I was for a while confused as to why anyone should believe such an obvious nonsense that there are no germs until I realised that the whole 'no germ' operation was a military psy-op.

I have yet to meet one orthodox, qualified medical doctor who believes that germs don't exist. There may well be a few but I've never met any. And I honestly don't see how anyone who understands the human body and health care could possibly believe such nonsense. Are there really any educated people arrogant enough to think they are more intelligent than Fracastorio, van Leeuwenhoek, Petty, Holmes, Fleming, Lister, Semmelweis and Snow?

And remember: those pushing the idea that there are no germs are allowed to remain on YouTube!

Many of those who claim that there are no germs have little or no understanding of the human body and have no practical clinical experience; they are, in short, ultracrepidarians of the worst and most dangerous kind. I understand that there is a very small, very vocal group of easily led people who want to believe that everything (everything) we have ever learned is wrong. These people believe that the earth is flat, that there is no gravity and that there are no germs.

The big mistake made by those who refuse to accept the germ theory is to ignore the overwhelming clinical and epidemiological evidence in favour of germ theory, in their desperate attempt to prove themselves cleverer than everyone else. There are, of course, other factors (such as the individual's environment and general health) involved in the development of infectious disease, and back in 1983 I wrote about the human body's astonishing healing powers which can have a huge impact on the way an infection may or may not develop, but none of those things proves that there are no germs. I sometimes believe that those who promote the notion that there are no germs (that there is no gravity and that the earth is flat) obtain their evidence from reading the entrails of chickens, studying tea leaves or tossing bones onto the floor. I've looked at the so-called scientific evidence which has been produced by those who claim that there are no germs, and the material they offer in evidence proves nothing of the sort and could be demolished in thirty seconds by a first year medical student.

I've spent five and a half decades questioning modern medicine but arguing that germ theory isn't valid is so stupid it just has to be a psy-op. There is no other explanation.

Individuals denying the existence of germs (probably controlled by the conspirators and the intelligence agencies) have lied about me, attacked me and threatened me. I get attacked more by the Conspirators and Globalists than any other doctor on earth. This has been going on for decades. And the folk who don't believe in the existence of germs seem to have decided to put the boot in too.

Every time I make a video the comments section contains gibberish from idiots who have no medical knowledge or experience whatsoever – but who are convinced that they are right and that there are no germs or infectious diseases. (Actually, I sometimes suspect that the vocal critics are probably just a relatively small number of people who pretend not to believe there are any germs. They are members of the CIA, use a hundred false names and spend all the days putting rude messages on anything sensible which they think could threaten the Great Reset.)

The UK's Online Safety Bill means that it is now illegal for anyone (including doctors) to question the Government's view on medical matters. So, for example, The OSB means that the authorities will officially be able to censor anyone telling the truth about the covid hoax. Questioning the Government can be punished with a five year prison sentence. Here's what one Labour peer, Baroness Merron, said in a debate about the bill: 'We all remember the absolute horror of seeing false theories being spread quickly online, threatening to undermine the life-saving vaccine rollout. In 2020, an estimated 5,800 people globally were admitted to hospital because of false information online relating to covid-19, with at least 800 people believed to have died because they followed this misinformation or disinformation.' Baroness Merron, who has a degree in management sciences and worked as a trade union official, was made a life peer in 2021. She was an MP for a while and is remembered for having expenses higher than average. She voted to support a bill to keep MP's expenses secret. Defeated at the general election of 2010, Merron is now Chair of Bus Users UK and Chief Executive of the Board of Deputies of British Jews. I have no idea where she obtained the absurd (and absurdly precise) figures she quoted (maybe she got them from Ferguson, the mathematical modeller) and since public debate about covid is not allowed, there is little chance of my ever being able to ask her.

I'm a qualified, experienced doctor who has been studying drugs, vaccines and iatrogenesis for over 50 years. Until 2020, I was widely considered to be a leading expert on such topics. Today, the Chair of Bus Users UK is the expert.

I hope, dear reader, that you begin to sense my frustration, my anger and my weariness.

During 2020, 2021 and 2022 my wife and I were working all the hours we could gouge out of every day to research and write about the covid fraud. We were, in particular, trying to stop the covid vaccine being given to children. And yet every video I made was attacked by the group who don't believe that germs exist. They lied, abused and threatened and made our lives miserable. What was the point?

The fanatics who believe there are no germs will go to great lengths to promote their point of view.

At one point, I was approached by an ignorant, deceitful, irrational and cruel fraudster pretending to be a publisher wanting to produce editions of a number of my titles. Since I had lost every foreign publisher I previously had, I found this offer cheering and said so. But it was a shabby trick and a complex fraud. Consumed by prejudice and irrational hatred for simple truths, which he couldn't comprehend or accept, this man went to a great deal of trouble and trickery to obtain my email address simply so that he could send me some of the pseudoscientific nonsense favoured by the 'there are no germs' idiots. In an attempt to soothe him I suggested, in vain, that we should both simply agree to differ. But you can never be soothing or logical with insane fanatics.

I've even had two quite seriously intended death threats from people claiming that there are no germs – fanatics who were quite unable to produce any evidence for their claims. And I suspect that it was the 'there are no germs' fanatics who cut through two of the tyres of a car we drive. The cuts were made to the inside of the front tyres and if one of the tyres had burst (as planned) we would have died – and so, probably, would other people.

And remember – some of those arguing that there are no germs are still allowed to share their opinions on YouTube. I think this is significant. As a general rule any writer or doctor who still has open access to YouTube, Facebook, Twitter, LinkedIn and any of the social media is surely not considered a threat to the Great Reset. Similarly anyone with a Wikipedia page which doesn't make them look like a combination of Ghengis Khan and Jack the Ripper is clearly being supported by the conspirators. My own long established Wikipedia page was suddenly torn apart and rewritten and stuffed with nonsense after I made a truthful video about covid-19 in March 2020.

The notion that germs don't exist is, in my view, in the same category as the idea that the earth is flat, the myth that global warming is real and the nonsense that vaccines are safe and good.

I believe the bizarre theory that there are no germs was designed to split what I think of as the resistance movement and to make people look stupid for supporting the idea. And it has been very efficient at doing exactly that.

I fear that the essentially doomed campaign to convince the world that there are no germs and no infectious diseases has torn the truth movement in half and destroyed whatever chance we had of defeating the dark forces of the conspirators. I firmly believe that the CIA has been responsible for promoting the idea that germs don't exist. The CIA knows darned well that the public will never take anyone seriously if they argue that there are no germs. Most people are only too well aware of the way that colds, flu, measles and chickenpox, etc. spread through families, schools and co-workers.

Here are one or two questions for all those who do not believe in the existence of germs:

1. If you ever need an operation (and I hope you don't) would you prefer the surgeon to wash his/her hands and used sterilised instruments to reduce the risk of infection?

2. Do you wash your hands before eating?

3. Do you wash your hands after you've been to the loo?

4. If you cut yourself accidentally (in the garden for example) do

you wash the wound and maybe put on a little antiseptic cream? Or just leave it dirty?

If you answered 'yes' to those questions then you believe in germs.

If you answered 'no' then you are, I'm afraid, a bit dim and not someone I'd want preparing food for me.

Those who don't believe in the existence of germs might like to explain the Great Plague. The plague was famously spread to the English county Derbyshire on old rags sent from London. Without the germ theory there is no rational explanation for how the plague devastated the village of Eyam or, more significantly, why the self-isolation organised by selfless villagers prevented the plague from spreading.

Oh, and one more thing: if there are no germs, why do antibiotics work (which they patently do).

The conspirators and the collaborators have complained that I doubted the existence of an AIDS virus back in the 1980s.

Back in the 1980s, AIDS was being used (just like covid-19) to terrify and control us all.

The entire medical establishment claimed that by the year 2000 we would all be affected. I campaigned ferociously against the lies (I was *The Sun* doctor at the time and had a number of other columns and regular broadcasting spots) and the AIDS myth collapsed.

(For the record, most of those in Africa who allegedly die of AIDS are actually dying of tuberculosis and are labelled AIDS patients to sustain the myth and the huge industry which grew up very rapidly.)

An article which I wrote in the 1990s, and which was published in 'Vernon Coleman's Health Letter' was used as evidence that I am an AIDS denialist. (What a strange word that is. Today, it is used so widely too.) Please note that the article was written around a quarter of a century ago. Would I write the same article now? I honestly don't know. I'd have to do a good deal of new research. But since this quarter of a century old article has been widely misquoted, it seems reasonable to include it here in full.

Since my Health Letter has been sadly defunct for some years, and since we delete old articles from the website every few years (simply to control the number of items) I'd forgotten this piece existed. This is perhaps not surprising since I estimate that I've published over 20 million words since I wrote this article.

Incidentally, I now suspect that the wildly exaggerated AIDS scare which terrified millions in the 1980s and 1990s (and resulted in many people committing suicide because they were so terrified of catching the disease) was the first attempt by the conspirators to create a fake global pandemic – and to help cut the size of the world population by discouraging sexual activity. It is worth noting that today, although many patients with other diseases, particularly tuberculosis, are officially listed as having AIDS, the total number of patients has never reached the figure predicted by the medical establishment, parts of which, I seem to remember, had predicted that everyone would be touched by the disease by the year 2000.

This reprinted summary seems to me to be a fair appraisal of what was known towards the end of the last century, and since so many enthusiasts, journalists and conspirators seem to be excited by what I wrote, and have mis-quoted it endlessly, here it is – completely as I wrote it a quarter of a century ago, unedited and unchanged. (Another appraisal of the AIDS scare appeared in my book *The Health Scandal*, which was published in 1988.)

'I have lately become convinced that the widespread notion that AIDS is an infectious disease, which is spread exclusively through sexual intercourse, is almost certainly wrong.

Back in the mid-1980s, I had serious reservations about the existence of a relationship between HIV (or, indeed, any causative organism) and AIDS.

In the late 1980s, I accepted the link between HIV and AIDS but rejected the theory, popular among the medical and nursing professions, politicians, journalists, insurance companies keen to find an excuse to increase their premiums, drug companies desperate to sell their latest AIDS related product, and just about every other scaremongering half-wit eager to jump on the 'AIDS is the biggest plague to hit mankind' bandwagon that AIDS was a sexually transmitted disease which was likely to wipe out a large proportion of the western world.

I argued that AIDS should be regarded as a blood related disorder, rather than a sexually transmitted disease, and that because of this it was primarily a disease that threatened homosexuals and drug addicts rather than heterosexuals. I didn't say that these were the only groups who would develop AIDS but that they would probably be the main sufferers.

The evidence shows I was right about that but I now strongly suspect that I was wrong even to accept that there was (or is) a link between HIV and AIDS.

The huge AIDS industry, now employing thousands of scientists, hundreds of thousands of administrators and paramedics and vast armies of sanctimonious fund raisers – as well as burning up billions of dollars of taxpayers' money which could have been much better spent on something useful – is now too committed to the notion that HIV causes AIDS even to admit that it might be false. But false it very probably is.

There have been around 400,000 AIDS patients in the last ten years. (The ground rules for defining an AIDS patients have constantly been changing in order to keep the number of AIDS victims as high as possible and, therefore, try to justify the expenditure involved.)

Those 400,000 patients have been treated by around 5,000,000 AIDS researchers and specialist AIDS medical workers. If the amount of effort and money spent on AIDS had been spent on teaching people how to avoid heart disease, millions of lives could have been saved and heart disease would now be something of a rarity among men and women under the age of 70. Since the early 1990s, most of the under employed AIDS experts have kept themselves busy doing their best to maintain the AIDS myth – the myth which has paid their unjustified and unjustifiable salaries. The AIDS industry – like the global cancer industry – is now predominantly composed of individuals whose primary concern is their own financial survival. The needs of patients – and the community at large take a poor second place.

Despite the money that has been spent, and the countless number of animals who have been sacrificed (in the US 1,500 chimpanzees which were bred for AIDS research and which, it is now recognised, have no useful function in the AIDS research industry, are kept alive in cages at an annual cost of something like $7,300,000), the AIDS industry has yet to make just one of the many promised breakthroughs or save any human lives. And that failure is probably due to the fact that scientists have based their research work on a premise with about as much supporting evidence behind it as the theory that the earth is flat.

AIDS was first noted in 1981 in the US. At the time it was described as GRID (Gay Related Immune Deficiency) because it only seemed to affect gay men. And it seemed most prevalent among promiscuous gay men. One early survey showed that the first 100 men with the disease had had, on average, no less than 1,120 sexual partners each. (Though how they each remembered the precise figure I can't imagine.)

None of the diseases associated with GRID were new. Some had previously occurred in drug addicts. And some observers wondered if the new syndrome had developed among these gay men because of their promiscuous, drug taking lifestyle.

But at the same time as doctors had identified the existence of what they thought was a new syndrome scientists had developed a technique to classify and count different types of lymphocytes – white blood cells and researchers noticed that some GRID patients had low numbers of particular types of white blood cell. It was, therefore, assumed that AIDS was infectious and caused by some sort of organism. And thus the AIDS syndrome was born. AIDS was never a new disease but merely an artificial syndrome consisting of several already existing diseases.

Surprisingly, it was upon this fragile theory that the whole AIDS industry has been built.

Naturally, everyone wanted to find the organism responsible for causing AIDS. When HIV was allegedly identified it was given this dubious honour, despite the fact that it was originally isolated in no more than around a third of AIDS patients. (Even today most AIDS patients do not have an HIV infection.)

The strange fact is that despite the billions that have been spent on research, the world is still waiting for someone to prove that AIDS really does exist. There is not and never has been any solid research linking HIV to AIDS – let alone proving that HIV causes

AIDS.

So, the big question now may appear to be 'What causes AIDS?'

But, in fact, I suspect that in truth that isn't the big question at all.

In reality, I suspect that the big question is: 'Does AIDS actually exist?'

And I suspect that the answer is that it doesn't.

As I have already pointed out, AIDS is a syndrome which does not consist of any new symptoms or diseases.

And in order to justify the huge expenditure of time and money on research into finding a cure, many of those involved in helping to maintain the AIDS industry have for years been busily changing the rules about the way that AIDS is defined. These days if you die of influenza or tuberculosis, there is a good chance that you will be included in the AIDS statistics. (Including TB victims in the AIDS statistics is one of the ways in which the alleged AIDS plague in Africa has been created. This type of 'bending' of the statistics is nothing new. When the authorities wanted to give the impression that smallpox had been conquered by the vaccination programme, they attributed many deaths caused by smallpox to chickenpox – even though chickenpox is very rarely a fatal disease.)

I suspect that the immune system breakdown which, in 'developed' countries usually leads to a diagnosis of AIDS, is probably a result of any one of a number of factors.

The use of illicit and recreational drugs has been offered as one explanation but I suspect that the over use of prescription drugs (including, I fear, some of those which are usually recommended for the 'treatment' of AIDS) is probably just as significant.

Nutritional deficiencies, constant stress and a steady exposure to carcinogenic chemicals all probably help to explain why AIDS (and other immune system problems) are now so commonplace.

The AIDS syndrome is still commonest among gay men, drug users and haemophiliacs – all of whom are probably exposed to drug use of one sort or another. The available evidence – such as it is – supports my hypothesis as well as any other.

It is my view that the best treatment for AIDS is a powerful immune system reinforcement programme – similar to the one I recommend for avoiding and treating cancer and for avoiding and treating infectious diseases.

There is no doubt that the original predictions for AIDS have all been proved utterly wrong.

In the 1980s a spokesman for the British Medical Association warned that by 1991 every family in Britain would be touched by AIDS, and attacked me viciously when I quoted evidence supporting a less scary point of view. Other medical establishment groups jumped on the 'AIDS is going to kill us all so give us lots of money to try to find a cure' bandwagon and the official line was defended with unprecedented ferocity and an astonishing amount of self-righteous, sanctimonious venom.

The World Health Organisation forecast that 100 million people might be infected by the year 1990, and the Royal College of Nursing in the UK forecast that one in fifty people in Britain would have the disease by the early 1990s. As far as I know none of these groups has apologised for their absurd scaremongering and none has provided an explanation for the size of their error.

In addition, numerous organisations and individuals have, when applying for grants, made dramatic promises of 'miracle breakthroughs' and 'wonder vaccines' solely because they know that the bigger the promise the larger the grant will probably be.

I have explained how and why AIDS became so fashionable in my book *Betrayal of Trust*. I believe that gay pressure groups (working to make sure that AIDS did not become established as a 'gay' disease') were responsible for the initial development of the 'plague' myth. And that AIDS was then turned into a major scare through the efforts of insurance companies (eager to find an excuse to put up premiums), drug companies (keen to sell new products), doctors (keen to help drug companies), researchers (eager to get their hands on the vast amounts of money being raised by volunteers), religious groups (desperate to exploit an opportunity to suppress sexual activity outside marriage) and politicians (eager, as always, to leap on an opportunity to frighten the voters – since when voters are frightened it is much easier to introduce new, repressive legislation).

I stand by that account.

But when *Betrayal of Trust* is next reprinted I will make one amendment: I will point out that it is my considered view that the disease we know as AIDS doesn't exist and never existed.

AIDS is a unique invention of the late 20th century: a plague disease that never was and a warning to us all to ignore politicians and the drug company dominated medical establishment. Perhaps the most worrying thing about AIDS is my suspicion that the hypothesis I have expressed here will never even be acknowledged or discussed by AIDS experts, by people working in the AIDS industry or by the mainstream media.

AIDS has become a sacred disease. To question the motives of those involved in the search for a vaccine or a cure, or the treatment of alleged AIDS patients, is politically incorrect and utterly unacceptable.

My hypothesis fits all the known facts and can explain everything that has happened over the last two decades. But if this hypothesis goes unnoticed nothing much will have changed and the AIDS industry will be following a long established pattern based on a mixture of hypocrisy, expediency and commercial need.

Back in the late 1980s and early 1990s I was vilified for daring to point out that all the available scientific evidence showed that AIDS was not going to be the plague that killed us all.

However, the AIDS industry quickly learned that the best way to silence opposition is to ignore it. That they have done consistently throughout the 90s. And that is what I expect them to continue to do. The silence will disguise the truth.

(Please note again that this article was written in the 1990s and has been reprinted here exactly as it was originally written and quite unedited. It is reprinted because critics have used it to describe me as an AIDS 'denialist' – failing to mention when it was written or precisely what was reported.)

In June 2020, I recorded a video entitled 'Why is the BBC Peddling Fake News?' Here is the transcript:

'Here are two recent headlines from the BBC website:

'We have a pandemic of black people dying every day'.

And

'Raheem Sterling: The only disease right now is racism'.

These are obviously absurd and seem designed to stir up discontent.

Of course there are black people dying every day. There are white people dying every day too. It is a sad, inescapable fact of life that in the end we all die.

But the headline from the BBC seems to suggest that black people are the only ones dying. Are they suggesting that white people have found the secret of eternal life but are hiding the secret from black people?

The second headline 'The only disease right now is racism' is obviously nonsensical but it's worse than that – it is insulting to millions of people who are struggling with real, physical disease which threatens their very existence.

The BBC is quick enough to condemn people for what it calls fake news but I doubt if there is any organisation more guilty of misleading its audience than the BBC.

Here's a headline from the BBC website: 'Coronavirus: UK Exceeds 200,000 Testing Capacity Target.'

Go down to the sixth paragraph and the BBC admitted that only 115,000 tests had actually been carried out.

The BBC is, always, bending the way it presents the news to suit the requirements of the establishment.

In another item on their website the BBC printed a drawing of a man walking through a tube train and leaving footprints behind him. The suggestion seemed to me to be that it is possible to spread the coronavirus on your shoes.

Is the BBC seriously suggesting that we wear disposable galoshes as well as gloves and masks?

The BBC seems to delight in fact checking stories (though sometimes rather comically I'm afraid) so maybe they'd like to check this story.

The BBC is always appalling as a source of news but it has excelled itself during this bizarre, manufactured crisis.

You might have thought that the BBC would have invited one of the many doctors questioning the whole coronavirus hoax onto a radio or television programme to discuss things.

But as far as I am aware they haven't done so. (Indeed, the BBC later admitted that it did not allow anyone questioning vaccines or vaccination on any of its programmes.)

Maybe they thought it might upset the Government.

And with a review of the BBC licence fee they wouldn't want to do that, would they?

The truth is, of course, that none of this is new. The BBC has a terrible record when it comes to reporting things honestly and fairly.

It is, I think, now widely recognised that BBC journalists seem to have lost the ability to differentiate between 'news' and 'comment'. One independent think tank commented that 'the BBC pays lip service to impartiality but acts more like a political party with a policy manifesto.'

A survey of just under 40,000 people showed that 85% of Britons no longer trust BBC News to give unbiased political coverage and it isn't difficult to see why. Celebrities commonly speak out in support of the BBC and endorse its line on most things but it is difficult not to suspect that this is sometimes because they fear that if they don't then they will be ostracised and will no longer be offered well-paid acting or presenting jobs.

Here's an article which appeared on my website early during the fake pandemic:

'Despite the celebrity endorsements, nearly ten million Britons cancelled their TV licences in recent years.

Many of them were disgusted by the fact that the BBC has been bought by the European Union. In one recent five year period, the BBC accepted 258 million euros from the EU. Over the recent years the BBC has accepted huge quantities of EU money. I won't accept £5 from an advertiser or a sponsor or the EU because my independence is important to me. But the BBC has sold its integrity.

Inevitably, therefore, it is no surprise that the BBC is clearly biased in favour of the European Union. The BBC has for years been consistently pro-EU and before the Referendum it was clear that the Corporation regarded the very idea of leaving the EU as sacrilegious. Even though the Corporation is funded by a compulsory licence fee taken from a largely unwilling and often rather resentful electorate, the BBC has deliberately favoured the minority point of view in support of the EU.

In the months after the nation decided it no longer wanted to be ruled by a bunch of unelected bureaucrats living and working in Belgium, the BBC did everything it could to demonise Brexit and

Brexiteers. On the relatively rare occasions when Brexit supporters were allowed into a studio they were invariably labelled 'right wing' and treated as though they were in some way criminal. On the other hand, when Remainers were interviewed they were treated with great respect and introduced as though they were independent commentators.

It became quite well known that when the BBC arranged a programme with an audience then the audience would be packed with Remainers.

Every piece of bad news was (sometimes laughably) blamed on Brexit and every piece of good news was accompanied by the phrase 'despite Brexit'.

Studies of the BBC have shown an overwhelming bias against Brexit.

But this partisan approach to the news is not confined to Brexit and the European Union.

The BBC charter demands that the BBC is impartial and reflects all strands of public opinion. In return for this impartiality, the BBC is entitled to an annual licence fee (currently around £150). But the BBC is not impartial. On the contrary, it is a corrupt and traitorous organisation which has betrayed Britain and the British. I believe the BBC is in breach of its own Charter and no longer entitled to the annual licence fee. Far from being expected to continue paying money to the BBC, citizens of Britain are entitled to receive refunds for the money they have handed over in the past.

When Donald Trump was elected President of the United States of America, the BBC reported the event with sneery comments on his opinions, his political views and his personality. And when the BBC reported his policies on immigration, they did so as though they were eccentric and extreme, although every poll showed that a majority of Americans and a majority of Europeans agreed with Trump's policies. Whenever Trump is mentioned the disdain is almost palpable.

However, whenever the EU supporting Obama is mentioned, the BBC drools with affection – never mentioning the former President's crafty deceits and the broken promises.

Moreover, the BBC appears to have a deep contempt for populism; a movement which has become global and which worries the political establishment so much that they dismiss it in the same sort of tone which you might expect them to use for fascism or communism. Here again, the BBC's attitude is irrational for populism is defined as a movement that champions 'the common person' in preference to the interests of the establishment. Populism invariably combines people on both the left and the right and is invariably hostile to large banks, large multinational corporations and extremists of all kinds. You might think that an organisation which is paid for by the populace at large might have at least a little sympathy with their interests, needs and anxieties. But, no, the BBC has firmly allied itself with the ruling classes and the Europhilic establishment and has no time for licence fee payers who are concerned about mass immigration, overcrowding, relentless globalisation and absurdly ill-based 'green' policies which result in new laws which have pushed up energy prices so dramatically that millions of hard working people have to choose between eating and keeping warm.

Most people now recognise that the BBC represents a minority viewpoint and gives absurd amounts of airtime and respect to the high priests and priestesses of political correctness. This may be because, as one senior BBC figure has pointed out, the BBC has 'an abnormally large number of young people, ethnic minorities and gay people' on its staff.

The BBC is not a broadcaster it is a narrowcaster; a propaganda unit for the elite.

Not surprisingly, the viewing figures for many BBC shows have sunk dramatically, and in the last couple of decades the viewing figures for the BBC's news programmes have shown a decline that would have startled any broadcaster which did not have the State's authority to collect money from millions of unwilling citizens.

The position is now so bad that if the BBC loses its licence fee then it will die because it will be unable to find enough viewers prepared to subscribe to its services. If the BBC retains its anachronistic right to demand licence fees then the annual charge must rocket to counterbalance the fall in the number of people prepared to pay the fee.

If you listen to or watch any BBC programmes, do so with scepticism in your heart and mind.

Today's BBC is Biased, Bought and Corrupt.

Joseph Goebbels, the Minister of Propaganda in the Third Reich, would have been proud of the BBC.

The BBC now peddles fake news because it's the only thing the appalling staff know how to do.

The BBC is one of many organisations (and individuals) who spend much effort fact checking statements made by others. The BBC regularly describes itself as a news organisation but if it were to fact check itself it would have to conclude that this claim is inaccurate and misleading. The BBC is a propaganda unit not a news organisation.'

In 2023, the BBC set up a Verify Team to investigate what they claimed was misinformation and disinformation. It seemed to me that there was no little irony in this since I cannot think of any broadcaster in the world which has spread misinformation and disinformation with such enthusiasm.

In the summer of 2023, I challenged the BBC Verify Team (all of them) to a live television debate about every aspect of covid-19 and the covid-19 vaccine. I sent copies of the challenge to a number of people at the BBC including the Director General.

Naturally, the silence was predictably deafening.

I don't think their refusal to accept the challenge was simple cowardice – I think they're just very well aware that they would lose the debate and look like the ignorant and dangerous fools they are.

But, to me, they looked like cowards.

I have often written that the quality of health care today is worse than it was in the 1970s and probably worse than it was in the 1950s. This sounds extraordinary but the decline in the quality of health care is easy to measure. In the 1970s, a biopsy to find out if a breast lump was benign or cancerous took twenty minutes. Today, a patient will probably have to wait at least a week (and possibly six or eight weeks) to get the result of a breast biopsy.

On 9th June 2021, I made a video entitled 'Lies on the BBC will Result in Children Dying'. Below you can read the transcript. I have repeatedly challenged vaccine supporters to a live, public debate about the covid fraud and the toxic covid-19 'vaccine' on network television. Not surprisingly, no vaccine supporter has ever dared accept the challenge. But I can't help wondering: have Sridhar and Spring apologised yet?

The medical establishment and the mainstream media continue to ignore and suppress the evidence which shows that the covid-19 'vaccine' should have never been made available and should be withdrawn immediately. I have asked the official UK covid inquiry, currently being conducted at great expense, to look at the way the public was misled and valuable information was suppressed.

We will not know for some years how many people (including children) have been killed or injured by this toxic, experimental vaccine.

'As you know, the BBC is the most dishonest, disreputable, unreliable media outlet in the history of the world. It's ageist, sexist, bigoted, unpatriotic and as bent as a paperclip. Over the last year I have recorded a number of videos detailing their errors and distortions. One BBC presenter has even boasted that the BBC will not share the truth about vaccines – they deliberately suppress those who do tell the truth about vaccines and vaccination.

There is no secret about why the BBC is hiding the truth. The BBC has close links to the drug industry, the crooked, corrupt vaccine makers, and is, of course, desperate to keep its licence fee by sucking up to the Government.

Now it seems that deceiving adults isn't enough. The BBC is now deliberately lying to children.

On the 8th June 2021, the BBC ran an item headed 'Pfizer vaccine for children – your questions answered'.

The BBC put questions to someone called Professor Devi Sridhar, who is apparently Chair of something called Global Public Health at the University of Edinburgh. They have to put the word global into it, don't they? Presumably, to show their enthusiasm for Agenda 21. I'm surprised they haven't got the word sustainable in there too.

Professor Sridhar, an American academic, says: 'The benefit of getting the vaccine is that you don't need to worry about covid-19. It means you're likely to not infect your parents, the people you live with and your teachers.'

This wretched woman Sridhar, who will surely burn in hell, claims that the vaccine is 100% safe for children.

And she is really reassuring about the side effects. 'Some children experience similar side effects to adults – these include fatigue, having a headache, feeling generally unwell, but these cleared within a day or two. And it seems a small price to pay for actually being protected from the real disease.'

So let's take those three statements and analyse them.

First, she says that if you have the vaccine you won't be likely to infect your parents and the people you live with and your teachers.

Where did she get this from? Who is her medical advisor? The Queen? Dolly Parton? Dermot O'Leary?

Well, it's not what the NHS says.

The NHS says: 'you might still get or spread covid-19 even if you have a vaccine.'

In other words the vaccine doesn't stop you getting covid or spreading it if you do get it. What it does do, allegedly, is reduce the symptoms you might get. That's hugely different. What an unbelievably arrogant and stupid woman Sridhar is to pontificate about something she knows nothing about and clearly doesn't seem to understand.

Second, Sridhar says this experimental vaccine, which only has a temporary approval let us not forget, is 100% safe for children.

And that is a downright, 100%, solid gold, lie.

And for that lie alone this bloody woman should be hung, drawn quartered, boiled in oil and tarred and feathered.

Sridhar is lying to children who are susceptible and vulnerable and terrified out of their wits by a year of unremitting propaganda.

So, what's the truth?

The truth is that in America the data up to the 28th May 2021 for 12 to 17-year-olds shows that there have been 4,740 total adverse events including 117 rated as serious and four reported deaths. Two 15-year-olds died and a 16-year-old and a 17-year-old. Those are the confirmed deaths. There are others not yet confirmed.

And this grinning, ignorant Professor Devi Sridhar of the

University of Edinburgh says it's safe.

Well, you horrid woman, death isn't safe. Death is final. It means it's all over. And this experimental jab is safe like being run over by a bus is safe.

No healthy children have died of this year's remarketed flu. Children get very few serious symptoms from covid-19.

But in the US, at least four children have already died of the experimental jab.

Third, the stupid, stupid, stupid Sridhar, whose name should now be immortalised along with Myra Hindley and Rose West, is reassuring about the side effects. 'Just a bit of tiredness and headache'.

That is another absolute bloody lie.

There were 635 reports of anaphylaxis among 12 to 17-year-olds with 97% attributed to the Pfizer vaccine. And there were 40 reports of myocarditis and pericarditis due to the Pfizer jab.

And 16 reports of blood clotting disorders.

And what about pathogenic priming?

And the real risk of menstrual and fertility problems.

And all this, let us remember, for an experimental jab intended to reduce symptoms caused by the rebranded flu – covid 19 – a disease which kills mainly people over 80 who are already dying of something else.

What's Sridhar going to do next?

Tell children to eat deadly nightshade berries or pick nice colourful toadstools and eat them?

Make no mistake this Devi Sridhar is a menace to children. Her advice could result in millions of children dying. She should be struck off the medical register.

Except she can't be.

Because she isn't a doctor.

Presumably the BBC couldn't find a proper medical doctor to praise this toxic jab. So they dug up Devi Sridhar.

She has never syringed an ear or removed an appendix or written a prescription or made a diagnosis.

She isn't a medical doctor. I am. She isn't.

And believe me this woman does not know what she is talking about. She is the sort of charlatan that the BBC should be exposing in my view. The newspapers should tear her apart. But they won't.

Because they are all bought too.

And so this ignorant, arrogant woman will continue to spread lies that will lead to death, pain and agony.

The latest figures from the UK Government show that in the UK the side effects involved with this jab include serious neurological problems, heart attacks, strokes, blindness and many other serious disorders. I think it is an insult to the patients who have been damaged to describe their side effects as mild.

Kids, who have smaller, more vulnerable bodies, are being given the same toxic junk as adults but up until the end of May 2021, these jabs had been responsible for 4,406 deaths in the US and 1,213 deaths in the UK. The VAERS figure for US deaths is now 5,165 and rising fast. Those are official government figures and they are low because less than 1 in 100 adverse events in the US is reported, and in the UK it's probably between 1 and 10%. Many deaths have been ignored or dismissed as coincidental. There is a pandemic of coincidences. In the US there had been 1,214 cases of anaphylaxis. Horrifyingly, 14,986 had needed hospitalisation and there had been 34,474 urgent health problems. In the UK there had been 1,213 deaths caused by the jabs and 859,481 total adverse reactions. Many people have gone blind.

Those are all official government figures Ms Sridhar. The truth is that the total killed and injured by these damned jabs will turn out to be far higher than the figures I've given. The figures for Europe and the rest of the world are just as scary. Weekly deaths all around the world have soared as more and more people are injected with this toxic junk. Women everywhere are noticing changes to their monthly cycle. And that's crucial.

Over half of GPs said they would not have the toxic jab. In the UK, the Government has admitted that despite putting NHS staff – hospital doctors, nurses, porters and bureaucrats – under pressure at least 20% have refused to be jabbed.

Perfectly healthy children are probably no more at risk of dying of covid-19 than they are of being killed by lightning. No previously healthy child under the age of 15 has died of covid-19 in the UK. Most children have hardly any symptoms if they do catch covid-19. Why would you jab against something so irrelevant?

What the hell is going on? Well, we know the BBC is linked to the drug companies via the Bill and Melinda Gates Foundation, but what about this pathetically patronising Sridhar woman?

Well, just type 'Bill and Melinda Gates Foundation' and 'Edinburgh University' into your favourite search engine.

Or just type in Devi Sridhar and Bill Gates. Or take a look at Devi Sridhar and Wellcome Trust.

The same wretched little BBC programme – which I am told is now being shown in schools by moronic teachers who believe the BBC is a broadcaster and not a bought and paid for propaganda unit for the drug industry, also contains a quote from the BBC's paid misinformation expert, the equally wretched and disgusting Marianna Spring whose qualifications, for all I know, consist of an O level in domestic science and a bronze medal for the hop, skip and jump. Ms Spring says: 'Those who make anti-vax claims usually don't have a scientific or medical background.'

Now that is odd because I know a lot of medical doctors who are, by the BBC's definition, anti vaxxers. In fact I could find more doctors who oppose giving this toxic vaccine to children than she or the BBC could find supporting giving it to children.

There's another little challenge for you Ms Spring – to add to the other challenges I've offered the BBC – all of which have been rejected.

See how many doctors – real medical doctors – you can find who think giving covid-19 jabs to kids is a good idea and I'll find more who know it's dangerous lunacy.

And that probably explains why instead of finding a GP or a hospital consultant or some other doc with a stethoscope, to lie to kids they dug this Sridhar out of the cave where she presumably lives.

The BBC has betrayed us for a long time now.

But this is a new low.

Are they deliberately trying to kill as many children as possible?

That's what it looks like to me.

In March 2020, well over a year ago, I warned that this was all going to be about pushing vaccines onto the public. People laughed and sneered. But that's exactly what is happening.

There is no excuse for lying to children like this.'

Throughout the years of the covid fraud, a young reporter called Marianna Spring was the BBC's disinformation and social media correspondent. It seems that Spring was indeed a specialist in misinformation. It was reported that she had lied about her professional experience on a job application form.

According to a report in *The New European,* Spring 'embellished' her CV when applying for a job at an American news site in 2018.

When she was found out she assured her potential employer that she was 'a brilliant reporter'.

The editor commented to Spring: 'Telling me you are a brilliant reporter who exercises integrity and honesty when you have literally demonstrated the opposite was a terrible idea.'

It was extraordinarily arrogant of Spring to assume that she would never be found out but it seems that hubris was not something Spring has ever lacked.

As far as I know the BBC did not mention Spring's personal exercise in misinformation on their website and they appear to have ignored the deceit.

I can only assume that Spring still holds her post as the BBC's misinformation specialist. How appropriate. And what utter hypocrisy.

Neither Spring nor the BBC can ever again dare to assume the moral high ground.

If Spring ever tries to interview anyone ever again they will, if there is any sign of a sticky moment approaching, bring up her deceit.

Spring claims to receive a good deal of abuse online (though I suspect she receives only a tiny fraction of the abuse I receive – much of it as a result of BBC programmes).

Her failure to give airtime to those of us providing scientific information about covid and the covid-19 vaccine suggests to me that her boast that she is a 'brilliant reporter' was unfounded – though the BBC may well consider her to be a brilliant propagandist.

If I am ever sued for libel, and have to find a lawyer then I will bring several hundred libel actions against the newspapers, broadcasters and individuals who have claimed that I am not a doctor, have been struck off the medical register, etc. I suspect that the money I win from those lawsuits will more than cover the cost my defence fees.

I reckon I have been libelled several hundred times by book reviewers (as the author I am not allowed to comment on libellous remarks or to defend myself against wild inaccuracies). In the days when reviews were confined to newspapers and magazines, it was possible to write a letter of correction to the editor – and to expect it to be printed.

I have repeatedly been accused of making videos to make money. This was, is and always will be a lie.

Making videos has cost us an enormous amount of money (not for equipment since we used an old iPad and a microphone which cost under a tenner) but because of huge amounts of money we have paid for books, scientific papers, etc. The biggest cost, however, has been the damage done to my income as an author.

When I first started making videos for YouTube (and subsequently for BrandNewTube, for Bitchute and for my own video platform on www.vernoncoleman.org) we had two rules.

First, no video would ever be monetised. I didn't want adverts over which I had no control appearing alongside my videos. (I seem to remember, however, that YouTube used to put entirely inappropriate adverts from the Government underneath my videos.)

Second, I always made it clear that anyone who wanted to, could make copies of my videos and, if appropriate, make translations. The only stipulation was that the videos should not be cut and be shown as they had originally been shown.

I've also refused to accept adverts on my websites or to allow any sponsorship. And because I always wanted access to my articles to be available to as many people as possible I never charged any fees for website material.

My only income comes from the online sale of my books. Because of bans, shadow-banning and suppression this has fallen by around 75% since the start of 2020. My income from foreign rights, once my main source of income, is now virtually nil.

'The difficult task is to enact only laws that are needed, to remain faithful to that truly basic principle of society, to be on guard against the passion for ruling, the most fatal disorder of modern states.' – Mirabeau the elder from `On Public Education'.

My telephone has been tapped for at least 40 years. Whenever we moved home – even in deserted country areas – a BT van would be parked outside for a couple of days. If we questioned the men inside the van, they would simply say that they were checking the line – even though no one had reported a fault.

Our phones would replay messages and our fax machine would buzz constantly as messages were taken from it and copied. Whenever we managed to find the number which had called us, BT engineers always said they would find out what was happening. They always failed except on one occasion when they managed to trace the number which had been sucking faxes off our machine. I rang the number and found myself talking to a very startled man in a room at Aldermaston …

People I knew (who worked for SIS) confirmed that Special Branch and GCHQ had been targeting me for decades

I used to attend and speak at a number of animal rights rallies in the 1970s, 1980s and 1990s and whenever I did so, I would be followed everywhere by a policeman with a video camera. (This caused considerable confusion whenever I talked to the lovely man who was running the ALF at the time. He, of course, also had a policeman with a video camera and so there would be four of us in a huddle.)

It has on several occasions been suggested to me that I should use encrypted emails or should use a VPN to protect my privacy. Since everything I have to say ends up in a book or on my websites I cannot see much point in this. Besides, if I use some sort of encrypted email service and the security services see this, they will assume that I am sharing secrets and they will demand access. If I refuse to give them passwords, they will obtain the information they want from whichever hosting company I use. Believe me, there is no privacy online. It is safest to assume that everything written in an email, for example, is as public as if it were written in the sky or scrawled on a wall outside your local police station.

Over the years I have received a number of threats (including more than my fair share of death threats).

After Interpol had spent many fruitless months investigating a clearly serious threat which came from Maltese hunters (objecting to my exposing their hobby of netting and killing millions of migrating song birds) I gave up reporting threats to the authorities.

Since I started writing and speaking about the covid fraud, I have received one serious legal threat (from a lawyer representing a doctor) and a number of physical threats.

In early 2023, two brand new tyres on our car were cut down to the point where they were dangerous. The cuts were made on the inside of both front tyres, in places where they would not be noticed, and it was only thanks to the fact that the car was being serviced shortly after the damage was done, that a very serious accident was avoided.

When I first started making videos I used to allow people to put comments on my videos. I had to abandon this when the comments section was swamped with abusive comments from the conspirators and their paid representatives. These were augmented by absurd comments from people who still hadn't learned to write their names or tie their shoe laces but who had a friend who could read to them, and who were able through some strange form of osmosis to consider themselves medical experts.

I discovered that if you argue with the bullies and the trolls, they quickly take offence and turn themselves into victims.

'Oh dear,' they cry, 'he has been rude to me. Boo hoo. I'm going to complain to teacher, Ofcom, the Government, the police or the site owner. Or, probably, all of the above.'

So I gave up trying to confront the crazed lunatics who were taking over the comments section. And, eventually I decided that the trolls and the bullies are best dealt with in the same way that rowdies and street bullies are dealt with – by ignoring them. After all, the value of a comment depends entirely on the perceived wisdom of the person making the comment.

It would be best for us all if the trolls and bullies were to go somewhere else, or to scrawl their graffiti on the walls of the nearest railway embankment – preferably standing back to view their handiwork just as a train is coming.

In 2022, Google was the winner of the Hypocrisy Gold Medal – overtaking Bono, His Royal Hypocrite, and the Duke and Duchess of California.

Google (the presumably proud owner of YouTube) was running huge ads announcing 'Digital attacks are being used to censor critical information online.'

The sly hypocrites created something called 'Project Shield' which they claimed was to 'defend journalists and organisations and more from these attacks'. Have you ever heard of such brass nerve?

Google and YouTube were, are and will probably continue to be the world's worst enemies of freedom, free speech and information. YouTube has for years been supressing the truth and censoring and banning truth-tellers. Google is, in my view, the most evil and hypocritical company on the planet beating even Goldman Sachs and Monsanto.

If more people had pointed out that doctors and journalists refuse to debate the alleged covid-19 pandemic, and the danger of the covid-19 jabs, the whole damned fraud would now be over.

The war we've been fighting was always a propaganda war and right from the start (best part of four years ago) I tried to shame the opposition, and awaken the public, by pointing out how truth-tellers had been silenced and the truth suppressed.

Sadly, the general view appears to have been: 'What's the point in demanding a debate, they won't give you one.'

But that was the whole point.

We could have won this war if more people had pushed hard for the public debate they were never going to give us, shamed the conspirators and their servants and made it clear to the public that those promoting the fake pandemic, the climate change fraud and the Great Reset had something to hide.

I reckon that over 100 of my over 300 original videos are permanently missing in action – removed by truth crushing employees at YouTube and then hacked out of existence at BrandNewTube. When my videos on YouTube disappeared (just a couple of months after I'd started the channel) I had around 220,000 subscribers and many millions of views. When my original channel at BNT disappeared I had around 75,000 subscribers and well over five million views.

For many months in 2020, Antoinette and I researched, wrote and recorded a video most days of the week. We literally did nothing else (well, we ate and slept occasionally but we took no holiday and no days off because we recognised from the start that this was a war we had to win). When daily videos become too much and were seriously affecting our health, we cut back a little. We have also researched and written thousands of articles for the Web.

Our reward has been that my reputation and our income have been destroyed and I have received a good deal of personal and professional abuse.

I'd like to record that, for whatever future might await us all, my wife Antoinette has, despite needing to take daily medication for two serious health problems, devoted most of her energies to this war for the best part of four years. If people were given honours for public service above and beyond the expected then Antoinette would be at the top of the list.

The woke have now apparently decided that criticising the 'woke' should be regarded as a form of racism.

Children don't know what is happening to them. They don't have any point of reference because they have been brainwashed by climate and covid lefty loonies masquerading as teachers. And, of course, social media is controlled by a far left wing conspiracy which bans all truths which stand in the way of the plan for a 'new normal' (which is jargon for 'new abnormal'). Anyone who isn't a rabid communist, far to the left of Marx and the BBC, is, children are taught, a far right extremist who must be silenced.

A seemingly endless number of television programmes have been made exposing corruption in football and other sports. But as far as I know, no TV company has dared make a television programme about corruption in the medical establishment and, in particular, about the unhealthy relationship between the medical establishment and the pharmaceutical industry. The only TV programme I am aware of which tackled this topic was one made by BBC1 in 1975 and based on my book *The Medicine Men*. Today, the medical establishment and the drug industry are far too powerful to be criticised. And TV companies are far too wimpy too try.

'Science without conscience is the ruin of the soul.' – Rabelais

In June 2021, I wrote and recorded a video warning about the end of the internet as we know it. It was, I fear, greeted with the usual jeers and disbelief. But as the internet comes under increasing attack, it seems timely to remember my warning.

The uncontrolled websites and independent platforms are the one remaining threat to the New World Order and they are doubtless a serious irritation.

Much to their annoyance, the conspirators are finding difficulty in suppressing the independent voices of those sharing the truth.

My own websites each receive many thousands of deliberate hacking attempts every month. These are serious attempts to take down the websites. It appears that the hacking attempts originate mainly with the governments of the US, Canada, Australia and the UK. As I have described in previous videos, they have done just about everything imaginable to silence me – with governments using lies and libels to try to discredit me. I have recently had email accounts mysteriously stop working. My WiFi works intermittently and very poorly (despite our having good equipment). My videos are always difficult to upload and often unusually difficult to find – that's one of the reasons why the transcripts of all my videos were for quite a while available on www.vernoncoleman.org (Now that my .org website has gone, my videos can be found via www.vernoncoleman.com which takes readers to my accounts on bitchute and onevsp.com though many of the 'views' were deleted on the latter platform by hackers.)

When my website www.vernoncoleman.org went, we arranged for visitors to the site to be redirected to www.vernoncoleman.com But the redirect didn't work properly and, quite possibly, still doesn't work well.

The old platform Brand New Tube was subjected to serious attacks. Muhammad Butt, who ran the platform, was told that if he allowed me to continue making my videos, then Brand New Tube would be taken down. He moved the platform abroad to avoid the UK authorities but the site was attacked and my videos on BNT were still taken down.

Those of us in the vocal resistance movement are doubtless regarded as a major threat by those who are attempting to introduce the thoroughly evil and undemocratic Great Reset.

It would be remarkably easy to shut down the internet and even easier to close down the parts we use – leaving the big commercial sites to continue operating.

Not possible?

Why not?

Even big websites have been hacked and shut down.

That's how vulnerable the internet is – and how easy it is to shut down specific parts of the whole enterprise.

The cloud – which provides masses of servers for customers everywhere – is supposed to help absorb changes in demand as well as putting users in contact with servers closer to where they are.

But much of the world's cloud is provided by just a handful of content delivery networks. It wouldn't be difficult to take down one or two of those –or to threaten to. It wouldn't be difficult to put pressure on them to exclude platforms or websites which carry what the enemy think of as subversive material. It would be easy to provide priority to the big commercial sites. It would be very easy to explain that independent platforms have to be shut down to protect national security. New laws are constantly being introduced which make this easy to do, allegedly in the national interest.

It's pretty obvious that the internet is incredibly vulnerable to the actions of people driven by a yearning for money and power – the very evil people behind the New World Order, the Great Reset and Agenda 21.

Ransomware – in which countries and big companies have to pay out huge sums to take back control of their networks – is booming. Government agencies reckon that criminal hackers pose a bigger threat to UK security than hostile states.

And I'm afraid that there really can't be any doubt that we are getting very close to the point where the crooks behind the Great Reset, supported by naïve and misinformed global warming campaigners, and greens who either have no real idea what is going on or who welcome the disappearance of freedom and democracy, will decide that the resistance movement needs to be shut down completely.

They're already desperately annoyed about our exposing the dangers of the experimental vaccine. I've noticed that whenever I do a video about the experimental jabs, the analytics change and people find it difficult to view the video.

You think it's unlikely that anyone would dare ban huge chunks of the internet?

You don't think they would do that?

I'm afraid those sentiments don't work anymore.

Who would have thought they would have dared lock up whole nations and destroy the global economy?

The people behind this fraud have deliberately killed millions of people and if we don't stop them they will kill billions.

There isn't anything they wouldn't do.

So, believe me, if and when they feel it is necessary to close down the whole internet, they'd do it without hesitation. And so they'll certainly close down the bits which they consider a nuisance.

To whom are you going to complain if your favourite sites disappear? How are you going to do it?

We have to be prepared for that eventuality. Imagine the consequences. No Twitter. No Facebook. Some email facilities will go down. No independent platforms. And no independent websites.

If they think it necessary they will close the internet completely. They will find it incredibly easy to close down the parts of the internet which they find irritating.

And so we need to investigate other forms of communication. We need to find new ways to keep in touch with one another.

'If Liberty means anything at all it means the right to tell people what they do not want to hear.' – George Orwell

The majority of journalists and some members of the public tend to regard the peer review system as a vital part of the scientific process.

If a new piece of research is published they will dismiss it as worthless if it hasn't been 'peer reviewed'.

I've got bad news for them.

The peer review system is not just worthless – it is dangerous and designed to perpetuate errors, misconceptions and faulty reasoning. Peer reviews merely confirm that a bunch of people with the same prejudices and commercial loyalties agree with one another.

The problem is that the 'peers' who are chosen to 'review' a scientific paper or a piece of scientific research will invariably be members of a small group of individuals who are committed to supporting the establishment – and who almost certainly have financial links to the establishment. If they are peer reviewing a medical paper they will, in 99 times out of 100, have links to the pharmaceutical industry.

Scientists who are asked to review a piece of research will be part of the system they are reviewing. They will depend for their livelihood on reputations built on supporting the establishment. The scientist who doesn't do what he is expected to do, and who welcomes original thinking, will soon be exiled and find himself unemployable. His work won't be published in the standard journals. A scientist who questions accepted beliefs (however blatantly wrong they may be) will not be asked to 'peer review' anything.

And the problem, of course, is that the pharmaceutical industry is known to be riddled with corrupt people and corrupt practices.

Scientific research which is original, and of real value, will be suppressed if it is considered to be inconvenient to the pharmaceutical industry and/or the medical establishment.

There is no doubt that the peer review system will be used to suppress valuable new ideas and essential truths.

It is, for example, largely because of the peer review system that valuable, valid information about covid-19 and the vaccination programmes currently being promoted, is demonised by the media and the public.

It is thanks to the peer review system that four out of ten patients given drugs suffer side effects (some lethal) and why one in six hospital patients has been made ill by doctors. It is thanks to the peer review system that scores of allegedly thoroughly tested drugs have had to be withdrawn.

In a world where truth was of importance, the peer review system would be regarded as worthless and discredited; it is corrupt and serves merely to maintain the lies promoted by the medical establishment – which is, of course, owned by the pharmaceutical industry.

The conspirators were never going to take chances. They knew that once they had begun their campaign towards the Great Reset, they could not take any chances. And they knew that their propaganda campaign would be opposed by people who could see through the lies and the misinformation.

And so right from the start they knew that they would have to stamp down hard on anyone (especially doctors or media professionals) who dared to question the official line. The conspirators and their advisors had another trick up their sleeves: controlled opposition.

There were (and are) several aspects to this.

The crudest was to employ the branches of the military and secret services to attack and discredit the truth-tellers. In the United States of America the CIA has been extremely active in this area. In the UK, much of the work of disinformation, misinformation, demonization and abuse has been in the hands of the British Army's 77th Brigade. And so, right from the start, I suspect it may have been the 77th Brigade which was busy putting abusive and libellous remarks in the comments section underneath videos questioning the official line on the pandemic.

Whatever the source, the abuse was often crude and sometimes threatening. My videos were constantly full of comments claiming that I did not have a medical degree, that I was a fake and a fraud and even that I didn't exist. There was, for a while, a serious argument online that I didn't really exist but was a computer generated image. The support for this was based on the fact that I rarely re-crossed my legs during a video. There was also an argument that I must be a freemason because I had rubbed my head once. And a few bright sparks suggested that I had forecast the conspirators' plans with such accuracy that I must be a Rothschild.

A slightly more subtle approach was to hire individuals to pretend to be on the side of the truth-tellers. I suspect that at least half of those claiming to be 'truth-tellers' were actually working for the opposition. Some have ridiculously complex organisations (with associated groups here and links there) and they have often been hugely successful at collecting money. Some have collected vast sums from gullible supporters and, in some cases, big fees from drug companies.

And there were others who regarded the pandemic as a career booster and were careful enough and pliable enough to be allowed onto main stream television and radio stations where what they said could be directed or manipulated. (The real truth tellers were not allowed access to any main stream media.)

There is nothing new in any of this, of course. The authorities have always infiltrated pressure groups or those who threaten to cause disruption. I have always been very active in the campaign against animal experimentation and back in the 1970s and 1980s, when anti-vivisection campaigns were regarded as the major terrorism threat in the UK (MI5 and Special Branch admitted that the absence of outside, traditional terrorists meant that in order to justify their existence they had to find some alternative, and anti-vivisection groups were selected as the most suitable target). I remember that one group of five alleged extremists was arrested. Unfortunately, it was quickly found that four of the alleged extremists were actually representatives of various official groups (one was a member of Special Branch, one was an MI5 officer, one was a policeman and one was an undercover journalist). Only one member of the group was a bona fide animal rights activist. Initially, the activist was charged the very serious offence of conspiracy but the case quickly fell apart and was abandoned when the prosecutors realised that a conspiracy requires two or more individuals – you cannot change a solitary individual with conspiracy. This was not an isolated instance. It was common place to find that groups protesting or campaigning against animal experimentation had been infiltrated by those promoting or supporting vivisection – though the majority of the infiltrators were being paid, either by the Government or by the drug industry.

Sadly, despite my experience, I am pretty sure that I've still been taken in by some of those purporting to be on 'our side' in this war. The security services have a long history of clever infiltration and there are recorded instances of police officers living with campaigners for many years before being exposed as under-cover spies. Some of the controlled opposition will have been put in place by the security services while others are probably paid for by the pharmaceutical industry. (If anything happens to me the evidence I have accumulated will be released.)

Back in early 2020, I was already sceptical and suspicious of strangers. Today, my fears probably make me seem ever so slightly paranoid.

'When the group reaches the size of five, a traitor is a statistical inevitability.'
Stanislaw Ulbrecht (quoted by Larry Beinhart)

Today, the figures show that nearly everyone under the age of 25 is suffering from clinical depression. Many if not most are taking mind numbing medication (either tranquillisers such as the benzodiazepines or antidepressants) even though none of this medication will do them any good and will, indeed, do them much harm by slowing their thinking processes and numbing their minds. In Scotland, over a million individuals are taking prescribed anti-depressants.

Sometimes, I wonder if the most active collaborators (employees of the CIA, SIS, BBC, etc.) really believe the lies they are defending.

Do they ever wonder if they might, just might, be suppressing a debate which we should be having?

And, if they turn out to be defending and protecting a bunch of corrupt, greedy conspirators (which they are assuredly are) do they believe they will be protected from the consequences of the Great Reset?

Or, when the Great Reset becomes reality will the conspirators merely decide that the collaborators (many of whom currently hold positions of authority) are no longer needed? And will they simply get rid of them? Was that one of the reasons for the mRNA vaccines?

'**H**e's not gone. He's here, in this place, in this place he gave us. He's all around us and in us, and he always will be.' (Marion, the settler's wife, talking about Shane – the eponymous hero of one of the greatest stories ever written, and one of the greatest movies ever made. Shane' was written by Jack Schaefer.)

I have dealt with fact checkers in several previous books. The world is now awash with people who earn huge sums of money by describing themselves as fact checkers and criticising truth-tellers. Most of the so-called fact checkers have absolutely no medical or scientific qualifications and their judgements are worthless. They simply say what their sponsors want them to say. Three and a half years ago I used to complain about their judgements but in the end I decided I was wasting my time. For one thing there are hundreds of them, and complaining about their fake judgements was pretty pointless. You swat one out of the way and another half a dozen appear as replacements.

And I honestly doubt if any discerning reader takes any notice of anything they say.

Fact checkers are whores whose views are utterly without value. I have not yet found any fact-checker with medical qualifications or adequate experience. Nor have I found any who were not paid by the fraudsters and therefore biased and worthless.

I have had a website presence since shortly after the World Wide Web appeared towards the end of the 1980s. I opened my first website in the early 1990s (1992) when it became possible to purchase domain names. (That's how I come to own all the most suitable domain names.)

In the early years of the 1990s, the most frequent visitors to www.vernoncoleman.com were the CIA, the FBI and various parts of the American military.

Today, I have to pay substantial sums to protect my websites from hackers – most of whom come from Canada, the United States of America and North Korea.

Each month my two main websites www.vernoncoleman.com and www.vernoncoleman.org suffer between 5,000 and 6,000 hacking attempts. The figure is never lower than this and is sometimes substantially higher. Nefarious individuals sometimes add to the excitement by sending masses of emails. I once had over 10,000 emails from a single individual over a weekend. You will possibly not be surprised to hear that I guard my address, phone number and email addresses with some caution.

Today, only www.vernoncoleman.com is left.

I have no idea how long www.vernoncoleman.com will remain active. It is constantly under serious attack and sometimes doesn't work as well as we would like it to. But, as I write, it is still there – and has been there on the Web since 1992.

I made well over 300 videos about covid-19 and the vaccine and the Great Reset. Some of them can still be found on my channels on www.onevsp.com and on www.bitchute.com which can be accessed from www.vernoncoleman.com

During 2023, doctors were shocked by the number of patients they were seeing who were suffering from Guillain-Barre syndrome – a serious neurological disorder which used to be fairly uncommon but which had, since the introduction of the covid-19 vaccine, become increasingly common.

No one should have been surprised.

If doctors had bothered to look at the FDA's list of the side effects they expected to see with the covid-19 vaccine, they would have noticed that Guillain-Barre syndrome was at the top of the list.

I first revealed the existence of the list on 8th December 2020 in a video entitled 'Covid-19 Vaccine Possible effects'. (The transcript of that video appears on pages 286-289 of my book entitled 'Covid 19:

The Fraud Continues')

If I knew, back in December 2020, that individuals who were given the covid-19 vaccine would be more likely to develop Guillain-Barre syndrome, why was it such a surprise to doctors in the summer of 2023?

Why had the mainstream media still not noticed the connection?

And why was the NHS still telling people that the covid-19 vaccine is safe and effective when the evidence long ago proved conclusively that it is neither?

There has been a surge in type 1 diabetes among children and teenagers.

A survey of 38,000 young people (reported in the *Journal of the American Medical Association*) showed that the rise is substantial.

Doctors are said to be confused.

They shouldn't be. I warned that this would happen. And I warned that the covid-19 jab would push up blood sugar levels.

Here's a list of the adverse effects which I warned would be caused by the covid-19 'vaccine'. (This list appeared in a video I made in December 2020.)

Guillain-Barre syndrome
Acute disseminated encephalomyelitis
Transverse myelitis
Encephalitis
Myelitis
Encephalomyelitis
Meningoencephalitis
Meningitis
Encephalopathy
Convulsions
Seizures
Stroke
Narcolepsy
Cataplexy
Anaphylaxis
Acute myocardial infarction

Myocarditis
Pericarditis
Autoimmune disease
Death
Pregnancy, Birth outcomes
Other acute demyelinating diseases
Non anaphylactic allergy reactions
Thrombocytopenia
Disseminated intravascular coagulation
Venous thromboembolism
Arthritis
Arthralgia
Joint pain
Kawasaki disease
Multisystem inflammatory syndrome in children
Vaccine enhanced disease

Look down the list and you will see 'autoimmune disease'.

Now, key the words 'diabetes' and 'autoimmune disease' into a friendly search engine.

And you will see that type 1 diabetes is an autoimmune disease.

I rest my case.

Quad erat demonstrat.

The epidemic of type 1 diabetes is caused by the covid-19 vaccine.

And the drug companies will now get ever richer selling treatments for diseases the drug companies caused.

Stalin is clearly a role model for the lefty, lefty pro-Great Reset, pro-EU, pro-climate change, pro-vaccine lunatics who are trying desperately hard to run the world.

The conspirators love to blame the 'extreme right' for everything bad that happens.

In reality, it is the 'extreme left' who are responsible for creating the designer war with Russia, for introducing crazy sanctions which will kill hundreds of millions and for insisting that the world heads towards the apocalyptic net zero they love so much.

From the minute it was invented, I argued that 'long covid' was not a specific disease and did not exist. I pointed out that patients who have suffered from the flu frequently have aches and depression afterwards. These symptoms commonly appear with virus infections.

It was, however, clear that long covid was being promoted as a useful way to allow people to stay at home and avoid going back to work. Within months there were, allegedly, many millions of long covid sufferers – huge numbers of whom were told that they would never be able to return to work. By the start of 2023, around 65 million people around the world were reported to be 'suffering' from long covid – a disease which researchers have shown doesn't exist.

Long covid was part of the plan to destroy productivity, to destroy economies, to increase vaccine uptake, to be used as a cover for vaccine injuries and to lead us into the Great Reset.

Today, a growing number of doctors around the world agree with me; denying that long covid exists or ever existed.

'If you do not change direction, you may end up where you are heading.' – Lao Tzu

In September 2023, I received a note from the NHS telling me that I should have my seasonal covid-19 jab. The NHS says that my 'health record suggests you may be at increased risk due to a health condition or medical treatment'. (The deadly covid jab is now clearly planned to be at least an annual event.) Well, I may well have a health condition. Or two. Who knows? But the NHS has no record of my having a 'health condition' and I am not receiving treatment. And so the NHS appears to be lying to try to trick me into being jabbed with an entirely useless and toxic substance. Why am I not surprised? Oh, and they also tell me that I may be eligible for one of their wonderful new flu vaccines. Sadly, there was no mention of a free toaster too.

A couple of days later, Antoinette, my wife, received an invitation to have her covid-19 vaccination. The NHS message said: 'This vaccine has a proven safety record.'

Now that was a blatant lie. The vaccine, rather than being proved safe has been proven to be dangerous and toxic. It has also been proven not to do what it was originally said to do. The covid-19 vaccine doesn't prevent you getting covid.

I then received an email from the NHS telling me to have a covid jab. The email was sent to a private address which had not ever been made available to the NHS.

A week after the email and the text, I received a letter through the post reminding me to have my seasonal flu and covid-19 vaccinations. (As usual the word 'flu' was all lower case but covid-19 was spelt COVID-19 to make me realise just how extra especially important it is.)

A friend of ours, well into her 80s, recently had her seventh covid jab.

When we asked her why, she admitted that she had the jabs only because she was constantly harassed into having them. 'I don't like them going on at me,' she said. 'So I get the jabs.'

A professor of Oncology, Professor Angus Dalgleish, has asked for a debate into the harmful effects of covid injections. 'As a practising oncologist,' he said, 'I am seeing people with stable disease rapidly progress after being forced to have a booster.'

When I first said this over two years ago I was viciously attacked by the media, the medical establishment and a variety of 12-year-old fact checkers.

The first forty or fifty years of abuse weren't too difficult. But the bans and the censorship and the demonization and the libels and the suppression and the threats and the abuse (from all sides) have begun to feel more than a little tiresome of late.

The worst aspect of it has been the effect it has had on my Antoinette. We've had much encouragement (for which I am eternally grateful) and received many kind messages but the abuse, the lies and the threats are truly debilitating. And the abuse, the lies and the threats from people who claim to be on the same side of this war are particularly hurtful and difficult to deal with.

Would I do it all again?

Of course, I bloody well would. It's what I do.

And what choice was there?

I used to be a Fellow of the Royal Society of Arts but, as I mentioned briefly a little earlier in this book, the RSA expelled me without a hearing or a debate or a chance to properly defend myself. They expelled me for daring to tell the truth about covid, for being 'mugged' by BBC television and for daring to question the global warming myth.

Everything I said and wrote was factually accurate and, as it becomes ever clearer that everything I predicted is coming to pass, I wonder sometimes if they feel just a little embarrassed.

Even if I had been wrong, what sort of organisation expels one fellow because one or two other fellows don't agree with something they have said?

My expulsion from the RSA was, at the time, rather a low point.

We both thought about death and suicide as the injustices mounted. The endless unjustified abuse made it difficult for me to leave the house or to meet people and made us both seriously depressed.

My wife is the kindest person I've ever met. In Paris I once saw her run across to a woman rummaging for food in a rubbish bin. Antoinette didn't just give the woman some money – she gave her all the money in her purse. All of it. I have known her to do that many times. She doesn't give coins to beggars or street buskers – she gives them currency notes.

I will never forgive the RSA because their mindless, censorious cruelty helped depress us both. It was, in some ways, a low point.

Antoinette was also a Fellow of the Royal Society of Arts. She resigned the day I was expelled.

The lack of debate and fairness has been commonplace throughout the years since early 2020.

None of the politicians, journalists, doctors, broadcasters promoting the official line has ever been prepared to debate their beliefs.

That is their strength, because it means that they can say and do whatever they like.

But it is also their weakness because it means that anyone who is thoughtful and fair-minded must want to ask the question: why have these subjects never been debated?

Like most countries, the UK is spending whatever money it has left on a hugely pointless enquiry into the way the Government handled the covid hoax.

Naturally, the inquiry is destined to last for years and provide a bonanza for lawyers who will make a fortune out of taxpayers.

It is unlikely that any questions will be asked about the lockdowns, the masks, the social distancing, useless PCR testing, pointless test and trace schemes, expensive Eat Out and Furlough programmes, the closure of schools and the pointless and dangerous covid-19 'vaccine'.

And naturally, those of us who told the truth about the fraud back in 2020 will not be invited to explain how we knew it was all fake.

Still, the UK Covid-19 inquiry has invited submissions from the public. The process is called 'Every Story Matters'.

I sent them this submission (included under their heading: 'Unfair treatment, for example, inequality, discrimination or harassment'):

'I am a qualified doctor. In February and March 2020, I pointed out that the covid threat was exaggerated. Later that year I warned that the covid vaccine would cause heart problems, myocarditis, blood clots, etc. and wouldn't work. Everything I said was accurate and later proved accurate. I was abused by the mainstream media and banned by YouTube and all social media for the modern crime of telling the truth. My attempts to debate these issues were met with silence. The BBC actually said that it would not allow anyone questioning the vaccine on any of its programmes 'right or wrong'. Thousands of lives were destroyed unnecessarily by the stifling of all debate. Freedom of speech is important and should be respected. My reputation and earnings were deliberately destroyed for the crime of telling the truth.'

I have also sent them copies of *Coming Apocalypse* and *Covid-19: The Greatest Hoax in History*.

If the lawyers at the Covid Enquiry really want to know what happened and why then they should read those books. I'm not holding my breath.

The lies about the covid-19 vaccine have done what I hope is irreparable damage to vaccination programmes around the world. In the United States it is reported that vaccine uptake is down by a quarter, and in the UK the Government and the mainstream media are circulating the usual lies and threats to try to persuade reluctant parents to have their children jabbed with the officially approved melange of toxic chemicals.

Free speech is today only available to those who say what they are told to say, or repeat what they expected to say, and who confine their remarks to topics and views with which the establishment do not find uncomfortable.

And anyone who thinks that is free speech is lost to the world.

I've always enjoyed Hilaire Belloc's work, ever since I read his *Path to Rome*. His book *The Servile State* is essential reading. Here is his definition: 'That arrangement of society in which so considerable a number of the families and individuals are constrained by positive law to labour for the advantage of other families and individuals as to stamp the whole community with the mark of such labour as we call the servile state.' There can be no doubt: much of the world now consists of 'servile states'. Here's how Belloc concluded his book (remember, he was writing in 1913): 'So far as I can judge, those societies which broke with the continuity of Christian civilisation in the 16th century – which means, roughly, North Germany and Great Britain – tend at present to the re-establishment of a servile status. It will be diversified by local accident, modified by local character, hidden under many forms. But it will come.' (Taken from *My Favourite Books* by Vernon Coleman)

Picking through the bullshit to find the truth is a messy and exhausting business. It is not an occupation I would recommend to the squeamish, the sensitive or the nervous.

However, although most things in life are equivocal, there are times when there is a clear line between right and wrong.

And you then have to decide where you stand – whatever the cost might be.

I've made two big mistakes in the last four years.

The first was to speak out and make videos about covid. That was professional suicide. Why the hell did I do it? It certainly wasn't for the money. I never monetised my videos or accepted any advertising or sponsorship money. And I never appealed for money through one of the fund raising websites.

'It had to be done and it was the right thing to do,' is the nearest I can get to an answer.

The second mistake I made was to use my real name. I should have called myself 'Avenging Warrior', 'Bigfeet from Brighton', 'Yankee Patriot' or one of those daft names which are universal among the people who write comments on the ends of videos.

Still, it's a trifle too late to change things now.

I have written a good many books on medical topics and I think it's time to stop. So this will hopefully be my last book on medicine, and it will certainly be my last book about covid-19, vaccines and the Great Reset. I really don't think there is anything else to say.

My sincere thanks to all those readers who have bought, read and, hopefully, enjoyed (or found useful) at least some of those books. And additional thanks to all those who left kind reviews on Amazon. I can't tell you how much difference those kind reviews make. At the very least they help counter the endless one star, abusive reviews from people who haven't looked at the book they 'review' – let alone read it.

Hopefully, I won't stop writing books. (It's as much a part of me as breathing.) But there are many subjects other than medicine...

Reading List

I have read hundreds of books and thousands of articles and watched a great many videos in the research, preparation and writing of my books, articles and videos. Below I have listed a few of the books I found most useful. (A similar, but not identical, list appears in my book *Their Terrifying Plan*.)

1984 by George Orwell
A cry from the Far Middle by P.J.O'Rourke
Agenda 21 by Ron Taylor
Animal Farm by George Orwell
BBC: Brainwashing Britain by David Sedgwick
Behind the Green Mask: UN Agenda 21 by Rosa Koire
Black water: The rise of the world's most powerful mercenary army by Jeremy Scahill
Blind Eye to Murder by Tom Bower
Bloodless Revolution by Vernon Coleman
Brave New World by Aldous Huxley
Climategate, The Marijuana Conspiracy, Project Blue Beam by the Dot Connector Library
Dangerous Ideas by Eric Berkowitz
Destiny of Civilisation: Finance Capitalism, Industrial Capitalism or Socialism by Michael Hudson
Dirty Wars: The world is a battlefield by Jeremy Scahill
Dynastic America and those who own it by Henry H Klein
Essays on Free Knowledge: The Origins of Wikipedia and the New Politics of Knowledge by Larry Sanger
Everything is going to get Worse by Vernon Coleman
Fifteen Decisive Battles of the World by Sir Edward Creasy
Fog Facts by Larry Beinhart
Greta's Homework by Zina Cohen
Hidden Dangers: How governments, telecom and electric power utilities suppress the truth about the known hazards of electromagnetic field (EMF) radiation by Captain Jerry G.Flynn
Hidden Persuaders by Vance Packard

Illuminati Agenda 21 by Dean and Jill Henderson
Living in a Fascist Country by Vernon Coleman
Love among the Ruins by Evelyn Waugh
Nobody Knows Anything by Robert Moriarty
None Dare Call it Conspiracy by Gary Allen with Larry Abraham
Notes on Nationalism by George Orwell
OFPIS by Vernon Coleman
Orwell on Truth by George Orwell
Parliament of Whores by P.J.O'Rourke
Politics and the English Language by George Orwell
Powershift by Alvin Toffler
Presstitutes: Embedded in the Pay of the CIA by Udo Ulfkotte
Say NO to the New World Order by Gary Allen
Science, Liberty and Peace by Aldous Huxley
Scrap the BBC by Richard D.North
Shaping the Future of the Fourth Industrial Revolution: A Guide to Building a Better World by Klaus Schwab
Social Media: Nightmare on Your Street by Vernon Coleman
Sold Out by James Richards
Stuffed! By Vernon Coleman
Technocracy: The Hard Road to World Order by Patrick M.Wood
The Art of War by Sun Tzu
The Collapse of Antiquity by Michael Hudson
The Creature from Jekyll Island: A Second Look at the Federal Reserve by G.Edward Griffin
The Dark Side of Camelot – Seymour Hersh
The Death of Money by James Rickards
The Fourth and Richest Reich by Edwin Hartrich
The Globalisation of Poverty and the New World Order by Michel Chossudovsky
The Greening by Larry Abraham
The Greening of America by Charles A.Reick
The Hidden Enemy: The German Threazt to Post-War Peace by Heinz Pol
The Lessons of History by Will and Ariel Durant
The Limits of State Action by Wilhelm von Humboldt
The Man Versus the State by Herbert Spencer
The New Germany and the Old Nazis byT.H.Tetens
The Octopus: Europe in the grip of organised crime by Brian

Freemantle
The Press by A.J.Liebling
The Revolt of the Masses by Jose Ortega y Gasset
The Rockefeller File by Gary Allen
The Shocking History of the EU by Zina Cohen
The Social Contract by Rousseau
The Social Credit System in China by Anonymous
The Tainted Source: The Undemocratic Origins of the European Idea by John Laughland
The Tycoons: How Andrew Carnegie, John D Rockefeller, Jay Gould and J.P.Morgan invented the American supereconomy by Charles R Morris
Tower of Basel: The Shadowy History of the Secret Bank that Runs the World by Adam Lebor
Trading with the Enemy by Charles Higham
Tragedy & Hope by Carroll Quigley
Unmasked: Inside Antifa's Radical Plan to Destroy Democracy by Andy Ngo
US-Imposed Post 9/11Muslim Holocaust and Muslim Genocide by Gideon Maxwell Polya
What happens next? by Vernon Coleman

Books on drug companies, covid and the Great Reset by Vernon Coleman

The Medicine Men
First published 1975, *The Medicine Men* was the first book to attack the drug industry and to draw attention to its unhealthy relationship with the medical profession.

Paper Doctors
When first published in 1977 this book caused a storm for Dr Vernon Coleman suggested that most medical research should be stopped. And he explained why in precise detail.

Betrayal of Trust
An analysis of medical practice, first published in 1994.

The Health Scandal
First published in 1988 and caused a storm. *Nursing Times* described it as 'central to the health of the nation' and the *British Medical Journal* described it as 'a book to stimulate and to make one argue'.

Coming Apocalypse
Published in April 2020, this was the first book to expose the fake pandemic.

Endgame: The Hidden Agenda 21
Published in 2021 this is a book about the future which has been designed for us by the United Nations, the Global Economic Forum and all those eager to further the aims of the Great Reset.

Proof that Face Masks Do More Harm than Good
First published in 2020 this short book is packed with research and does exactly what it says on the cover.

Social Credit: Nightmare on Your Street
An explanation of how social credit schemes will destroy your life.

A Bigger Problem than Climate Change
An analysis of the coming oil shortage.

Covid-19: The Greatest Hoax in History
The first and earliest collection of transcripts from Vernon Coleman's videos.

Covid-19: The Fraud Continues
The second collection of transcripts from Vernon Coleman's videos.

Covid-19: Exposing the Lies
The third collection of transcripts from Vernon Coleman's videos. Also contains articles from *The Light Paper* and from the websites.

They Want Your Money and Your Life
Truths you must know about the coming depression, economic war and years of crisis.

Their Terrifying Plan
Dr Coleman explains how insane billionaire globalists are plotting to take over the world. He describes the terrifying future they have designed for you, your children and your grandchildren and analyses in detail the way in which ruthless, greedy people have taken control.

Medical Heretics
How the medical establishment has always crushed the truth and suppressed good ideas.

A Needle for a Needle: A Mother's Covid Revenge
A novella about a mother who seeks revenge when her son is killed by a covid-19 vaccination.

NHS: What's Wrong and How to Put it Right
A short analytical and constructive appraisal of the UK's National Health Service

The Author

Dr Vernon Coleman MB ChB DSc has been writing about drug companies and the medical profession for over 50 years. His first book *The Medicine Men*, published in 1975, was the first to question the relationship between the drug industry and the medical establishment. Since then he has written over 100 books (including many international bestsellers).

In February 2020, he told readers of his website www.vernoncoleman.com that the risks associated with the coronavirus were exaggerated. At the beginning of March 2020, he explained how and why the mortality figures had been distorted. On March 14th 2020 he warned that the Government's policies would result in far more deaths than the disease itself.

In a YouTube video recorded on 18th March 2020, Dr Coleman warned that governments would use the fake 'crisis' to oppress the elderly, to introduce compulsory inoculation and to begin to replace cash with digital money.

He revealed that the infection had been downgraded on March 19th when the public health bodies in the UK and the Advisory Committee on Dangerous Pathogens decided that the 'crisis' infection should no longer be classified as a 'high consequence infectious disease'. Just days after the significance of the infection had been officially downgraded, governments around the world put millions of people under house arrest.

Dr Coleman was immediately banned from all social media (Facebook told him he could not join because he would be a threat to their 'community'). Publishers banned his books and articles. YouTube deleted his 'Old Man in a Chair' channel, removed videos with millions of views and even banned him from looking at other people's videos. He was demonised, lied about and libelled.

Throughout the dark days of the fake pandemic and the greater fraud, Dr Coleman issued a series of videos (often one a day) detailing different aspects of the fraud and the dangers of the covid-19 'vaccine'. His first video, released in March 2020, was called 'Coronavirus: the Hoax of the Century' and had many millions of views within 24 hours. Dr Coleman also wrote a number of books on covid and the Great Reset: including 'Coming Apocalypse', 'Covid-19: The Greatest Hoax in History', 'Covid-19: Exposing Lies', 'Covid-19: The Fraud Continues', 'Endgame', 'Social Credit: Nightmare on Your Street', 'Proof that Face Masks do more Harm than Good', 'They want your money and your life' and 'Their Terrifying Plan'.

Vernon Coleman's first book about the covid fraud, called 'Coming Apocalypse', was published in April 2020. It was the first book to be written about covid and the covid fraud. In 'Coming Apocalypse', Vernon Coleman explained that the hoax had been deliberately invented to kill old people, get rid of cash and introduce a programme of compulsory vaccination. Events showed these predictions to be absolutely accurate.

Despite the widespread bans and censorship, hundreds of millions have watched his videos and although he was undoubtedly the most banned doctor in the world tens of millions a month visited his websites, from countries all around the world. (A recent analytics snapshot from Cloudflare for www.vernoncoleman.org alone showed 7,901,769 visitors from the UK, 6,925,968 from the US; 1,814,978 from Canada, 1,710,055 from Germany and 8,595,223 from the rest of the world. These figures were for one recent month in 2023 and do not include the many millions of times articles were reproduced on other sites.)

Dr Vernon Coleman's other non-fiction books include 'Anyone who tells you vaccines are safe and effective is lying: Here's the Proof' and 'How to stop your doctor killing you'.

Dr Coleman, a former GP principal, is a Sunday Times bestselling author. His books have sold over three million copies in the UK, been translated into 26 languages and sold in over 50 countries. Prior to March 2020 he had published over 5,000 articles and papers in newspapers, magazines and journals and had written columns for dozens of leading newspapers and magazines around the world. He was the founding editor of the British Clinical Journal and founded and published the European Medical Journal. Numerous TV and radio series have been based on his books. His novel 'Mrs Caldicot's Cabbage War' (about the oppression and mistreatment of the elderly) was turned into a highly successful, award winning film which is still frequently shown on television. In the UK, he has given evidence about the pointlessness of animal experimentation to the

House of Commons and the House of Lords and his campaigns have over many decades changed Government policy. He campaigned against the overuse of benzodiazepine tranquillisers throughout the 1970s and 1980s and when the British Government took action to control the drugs the Minister admitted in the House of Commons that action had been taken in response to his campaign. Vernon Coleman has lectured doctors and nurses in numerous countries.

What the papers say:

'Vernon Coleman writes as a general practitioner who has become disquieted by the all-pervasive influence of the pharmaceutical industry in modern medicine…He describes, with a wealth of illustrations, the phenomena of modern iatrogenesis; but he is also concerned about the wider harm which can result from doctors' and patients' preoccupation with medication instead of with the prevention of disease. He demonstrates, all the more effectively because he writes in a sober, matter-of-fact style, the immense influence exercised by the drug industry on doctors' prescribing habits…He writes as a family doctor who is keenly aware of the social dimensions of medical practice. He ends his book with practical suggestions as to how medical care – in the developing countries as well as in the West – can best be freed from this unhealthy pharmaceutical predominance.' – G.M.Carstairs, The Times Literary Supplement (1975)

'What he says of the present is true: and it is the great merit of the book that he says it from the viewpoint of a practising general practitioner, who sees from the inside what is going on, and is appalled by the consequences to the profession, and to the public.' – Brian Inglis, Punch (1975)

'Dr Coleman writes with more sense than bias. Required reading for any Minister of Health' – Daily Express

'I hope this book becomes a bestseller among doctors, nurses and the wider public…' – Nursing Times

'Dr Coleman's well-coordinated book could not be more timely.' – Yorkshire Post

'Few would disagree with Dr Coleman that more should be done about prevention.' – The Lancet

'This short but very readable book has a message that is timely.

Vernon Coleman's point is that much of the medical research into which money and expertise are poured is useless. At the same time, remedial conditions of mind and body which cause the most distress are largely neglected. This is true.' – Daily Telegraph

'If you believe Dr Vernon Coleman, the main beneficiaries of the hundred million pounds worth of research done in this country each year are certainly not the patients. The research benefits mostly the medical place seekers, who use their academic investigations as rungs on the promotional ladder, or drug companies with an eye for the latest market opening…The future may hold bionic superman but all a nation's physic cannot significantly change the basic mortality statistics except sometimes, to make them worse.' – The Guardian

'Dr Coleman's well-coordinated book could not be more timely.' – Yorkshire Post

'The Medicine Men is well worth reading' – Times Educational Supplement

'Dr Vernon Coleman…is not a mine of information – he is a fountain. It pours out of him, mixed with opinions which have an attractive common sense ring about them.' – Coventry Evening Telegraph

'When the children have finished playing the games on your Sinclair or Commodore Vic 20 computer, you can turn it to more practical purposes. For what is probably Britain's first home doctor programme for computers is now available. Dr Vernon Coleman, one of the country's leading medical authors, has prepared the text for a remarkable series of six cassettes called The Home Doctor Series. Dr Coleman, author of the new book 'Bodypower'…has turned his attention to computers.' – The Times 1983

'The Medicine Men' by Dr Vernon Coleman, was the subject of a 14 minute 'commercial' on the BBC's Nationwide television programme recently. Industry doctors and general practitioners come in for a severe drubbing: two down and several more to go because the targets for Dr Coleman's pen are many, varied and, to say the least, surprising. Take the physicians who carry out clinical trials: many of those, claims the author, have sold themselves to the industry and agreed to do research for rewards of one kind or another, whether that reward be a trip abroad, a piece of equipment, a few dinners, a series of published papers or simply money.' – The Pharmaceutical Journal

'By the year 2020 there will be a holocaust, not caused by a plutonium plume but by greed, medical ambition and political opportunism. This is the latest vision of Vernon Coleman, an articulate and prolific medical author…this disturbing book detects diseases in the whole way we deliver health care.' – Sunday Times (1988)

'…the issues explores he explores are central to the health of the nation.' – Nursing Times

'It is not necessary to accept his conclusion to be able to savour his decidedly trenchant comments on today's medicine…a book to stimulate and to make one argue.' – British Medical Journal

'As a writer of medical bestsellers, Dr Vernon Coleman's aim is to shock us out of our complacency…it's impossible not to be impressed by some of his arguments.' – Western Daily Press

'Controversial and devastating' – Publishing News

'Dr Coleman produces mountains of evidence to justify his outrageous claims.' – Edinburgh Evening News

'Dr Coleman lays about him with an uncompromising verbal scalpel, dipped in vitriol, against all sorts of sacred medical cows.' – Exeter Express and Echo

'Vernon Coleman writes brilliant books.' – The Good Book Guide

'No thinking person can ignore him. This is why he has been for over 20 years one of the world's leading advocates on human and animal rights in relation to health. Long may it continue.' – The

Ecologist

'The calmest voice of reason comes from Dr Vernon Coleman.' – The Observer

'A godsend.' – Daily Telegraph

'Dr Vernon Coleman has justifiably acquired a reputation for being controversial, iconoclastic and influential.' – General Practitioner

'Superstar.' – Independent on Sunday

'Brilliant!' – The People

'Compulsive reading.' – The Guardian

'His message is important.' – The Economist

'He's the Lone Ranger, Robin Hood and the Equalizer rolled into one.' – Glasgow Evening Times

'The man is a national treasure.' – What Doctors Don't Tell You

'His advice is optimistic and enthusiastic.' – British Medical Journal

'Revered guru of medicine.' – Nursing Times

'Gentle, kind and caring' – Western Daily Press

'His trademark is that he doesn't mince words. Far funnier than the usual tone of soupy piety you get from his colleagues.' – The Guardian

'Dr Coleman is one of our most enlightened, trenchant and sensitive dispensers of medical advice.' – The Observer

'Vernon Coleman is a leading medical authority and known to millions through his writing, broadcasting and bestselling books.' – Woman's Own

'His book Bodypower is one of the most sensible treatises on personal survival that has ever been published.' – Yorkshire Evening Post

'One of the country's top health experts.' – Woman's Journal

'Dr Coleman is crusading for a more complete awareness of what is good and bad for our bodies. In the course of that he has made many friends and some powerful enemies.' – Western Morning News

'Brilliant.' – The People

'Dr Vernon Coleman is one of our most enlightened, trenchant and sensible dispensers of medical advice.' – The Observer

'The most influential medical writer in Britain. There can be little doubt that Vernon Coleman is the people's doctor.' – Devon Life

'The medical expert you can't ignore.' – Sunday Independent

'A literary genius.' – HSL Newsletter

'I would much rather spend an evening in his company than be trapped for five minutes in a radio commentary box with Mr Geoffrey Boycott.' – Peter Tinniswood, Punch

'Hard hitting...inimitably forthright.' – Hull Daily Mail

'Refreshingly forthright.' – Liverpool Daily Post

'Outspoken and alert.' – Sunday Express

'The man with a mission.' – Morning News

'A good read...very funny and packed with interesting and useful advice.' –The Big Issue

'Dr Coleman gains in stature with successive books' – Coventry

Evening Telegraph

'Dr Coleman made me think again.' – BBC World Service

'Marvellously succinct, refreshingly sensible.' – The Spectator

'The living terror of the British medical establishment. A doctor of science as well as a medical graduate. Dr Coleman is probably one of the most brilliant men alive today. His extensive medical knowledge renders him fearless.' – Irish Times

'His future as King of the media docs is assured.' – The Independent

'Britain's leading medical author.' – The Star

'His advice is practical and readable.' – Northern Echo

'The layman's champion.' –Evening Herald

'All commonsense and no nonsense.' – Health Services Management

'One of Britain's leading experts.' – Slimmer Magazine

'The only three things I always read before the programme are Andrew Rawnsley in the Observer, Peter Hitchens in the Mail and Dr Vernon Coleman in The People. Or, if I'm really up against it, just Vernon Coleman.' – Eddie Mair, Presenter on BBC's Radio Four

'Dr Coleman is more illuminating than the proverbial lady with the lamp' – Company Magazine

'Britain's leading health care campaigner.' – The Sun

'What he says is true.' – Punch

'Perhaps the best known health writer for the general public in the world today.' – The Therapist

'The patient's champion. The doctor with the common touch.' – Birmingham Post

'A persuasive writer whose arguments, based on research and experience, are sound.' – Nursing Standard

'Coleman is controversial but respected and has been described in the British press as `the sharpest mind in medial journalism' and `the calmest voice of reason'. – Animals Today

'Vernon Coleman…rebel with a cause.' – Belfast Newsletter

'…presents the arguments against drug based medicine so well, and disturbs a harmful complacency so entertainingly.' – Alternative News

'He is certainly someone whose views are impossible to ignore, with his passionate advocacy of human and animal rights.' – International Journal of Alternative and Complementary Medicine

'The doctor who dares to speak his mind.' – Oxford Mail

'Dr Coleman speaks openly and reassuringly.' – Oxford Times

'He writes lucidly and wittily.' – Good Housekeeping

A Small Selection of Reference Articles referring to Vernon Coleman (Included to counter some of the lies on the internet)

Ref 1
'Volunteer for Kirkby' – The Guardian, 14.5.1965
Ref 2
'Bumbledom forced me to leave the NHS' – Pulse, 28.11.1981
Ref 3
'I'm Addicted to The Star' – The Star, 10.3.1988
Ref 4
'Medicine Becomes Computerised: Plug In Your Doctor.' – The Times, 29.3.1983
Ref 5
'Computer aided decision making in medicine' – British Medical Journal, 8.9.1984 and 27.10.1984
Ref 6
'Conscientious Objectors' – Financial Times magazine, 9.8.2003
Ref 7
'Doctor with the Common Touch.' – Birmingham Post, 9.10.1984
Ref 8
'Sacred Cows Beware: Vernon Coleman publishing again.' – The Scotsman, 6.12.1984
Ref 9
'Our Doctor Coleman Is Mustard' – The Sun, 29.6.1988
Ref 10
'Reading the mind between the lines.' – BMA News Review, November 1991
Ref 11
Doctors' Firsts – BMA News Review, 21.2.1996
Ref 12
'The big league of self publishing.' – Daily Telegraph, 17.8.1996
Ref 13
'Doctoring the books' – Independent, 16.3.1999
Ref 14

'Sick Practices' – Ode Magazine, July/August 2003
Ref 15
'You have been warned, Mr Blair.' – Spectator, 6.3.2004 and
20.3.2004
Ref 16
'Food for thought with a real live Maverick.' – Western Daily Press,
5.9.2006
Ref 17
'The doctor will see you now' – Independent, 14.5.2008

There is a more comprehensive list of reference articles on
www.vernoncoleman.com

Final Note from the Author:

If you found this book useful or informative I would be very grateful
if you would put a suitable review online. It helps more than you can
imagine.
Vernon Coleman

Printed in Great Britain
by Amazon

32874076R00089